TALES OF NASRUDIN:
KEYS TO FULFILLMENT

TALES OF
NASRUDIN

Keys to Fulfillment

Translation
ALI JAMNIA

Commentary
ALI JAMNIA
CHARLES DANIEL
CHARLES UPTON

SOPHIA PERENNIS

SAN RAFAEL, CA

First edition,
first published in the USA
by Sophia Perennis
© Sophia Perennis 2006

For information, address:
Sophia Perennis, P.O. Box 151011
San Rafael, CA 94915
sophiaperennis.com

Library of Congress Cataloging-in-Publication Data

Tales of Nasrudin: keys to fulfillment
/ translation, Ali Jamnia; commentary,
Ali Jamnia, Charles Daniel, Charles Upton.—1st ed.

p. cm.

ISBN 1 59731 070 0 (pbk: alk. paper)
ISBN 1 59731 071 9 (hardcover: alk. paper)
1. Nasreddin Hoca (Anecdotes) 2. Nasreddin Hoca
(Legendary character) I. Jamnia, Ali, 1961–
PN 6231.N27T35   2006
398.2'09561—dc22   2006021561

CONTENTS

INTRODUCTION

This work is uniquely aimed at using a collection of what superficially can be considered as jokes for education and development of insight and at the same time to bringing two vastly different Eastern and Western cultures to a better understanding. To familiarize the reader with our approach and thinking, we each decided to express our views separately. There may be both agreements and contradictions between us as the authors. However, this is intended in the hope of involving the reader in our debate.

NASRUDIN AND THE WESTERN EDUCATION SYSTEM

It would be interesting to trace the influences in Western thought that have lead to the exclusion of humor in education. There is a case to be made that these influences stretch all the way back to the founding of the university system in Medieval Europe. However, since it is not the intention of this book to speculate on the history of education, let us state that for whatever reason, in Western education, humor was not and is not seen as a useful technique.

In other parts of the world, this is not (always) the case. From the simplicity of Aesop's fables to the Mulla Nasrudin jokes in this book, there has been an understanding of the use of humor as a way of by-passing the conditioned responses that impede learning. There is an interesting paradox here. While in the West, the Mulla Nasrudin collection is now seen as a useful tool, in its native lands of Eastern Europe and Central Asia, the collection is seen as little more than simple jokes. It is only after the jokes are unraveled that traces of their real elements are seen. The fact that these jokes confound many people who encounter them is in itself interesting.

Why is it that so many of us have lost our abilities of independent interpretation? Is it that our modern communications system based on the passive reception of information (as experienced through television, radio and a school system that demands rote memory) has caused a decay of our basic reasoning abilities? It is not difficult to see how such systems pre-program our interest and taste. A quick look at any popular television program (or movie) says volumes about what holds people's interest. Programs that either dredge up the cheapest emotions or cauterize the sensitivities are the rule and not the exception. Along with this type of programming one gets the typical conditioned response that excludes any type of real learning. If you try to point out someone's conditioning (i.e. their unthinking responses), you can be sure that you will receive a host of rationalizations which will generally end up with something along the lines of "that's just the way I am." Of course, there is nothing necessarily wrong with someone just because they are conditioned. However, when the conditioning leads to destructive behavior and the individual still defends it... well, there doesn't seem to be much anyone can do... no one except perhaps Mulla Nasrudin!

Confronted with an opponent standing in front of a trash heap and ready to fight to the death to defend their rubbish, Mulla doesn't draw his weapon and prepare for battle. Instead, he simply holds up a mirror and lets them see their true situation. His methods for doing this are as varied as the situations of life. Sometimes Mulla will imitate someone else's behavior. Sometimes, he takes a normal situation and stretches it to the extreme. All the while, he makes his opponent laugh.

This last is the most important point. It is very difficult to snap out of a conditioned response when one is laughing at how stupid Mulla is acting. It is generally only later that we realize that everyone (at some time) acts like Mulla Nasrudin. This process of laughing and then realizing something new is very important when one examines the short history of popular meditation in the West.

It should be noted that meditation systems have existed in the West for a long time. However since these systems have been largely confined to monasteries, it has been only in the last forty or so years that popular meditation (along with 'instant' enlightenment) has found a place in the free market. Of course, time has shown that the idea of 'instant and effortless' enlightenment is in reality just as silly as it sounds. Added to this is the obvious misunderstanding of what one must do to develop insight.

By whatever criterion we choose to judge a person's mental and emotional development, insight is very high (if not on top) of the list. This is important when one realizes that the majority of the meditation systems have nothing in their training methods through which one can develop new insights. There are, of course, systems such as Zen which make their central point an attack on the intellect, but they offer nothing to replace what they are so intent on removing. In fact, there is very good case to be made that the vast majority of 'gurus for hire' are so intent on removing thinking capacity simply because it gives them greater control of their flock (and their follower's wallets). This is not meant to be an indictment of everyone involved, but a rational individual might well ask if a person's unwillingness to answer reasonable questions is evidence that they cannot provide such answers. This said, where do Mulla Nasrudin and his simple jokes fit in?

By allowing readers to laugh, reflect and hopefully see themselves in a new light, Mulla will help bring about new insights without the need for expensive gurus, changes in diet, dress, behavior and who knows what else. Of course, Mulla himself would not claim that simply reading his stories is enough to totally develop a person's capacities. He might also point out that in many cases his own style of teaching is not even necessary. However, we suspect that he would also claim that by reading (and occasionally re-reading) about his adventures, certain readers might be able to take some real steps and enjoy the journey along the way.

HISTORICAL AND CULTURAL NASRUDIN

In the ancient cultures in general, and in the cultures of East and Middle East in particular, stories were given tremendous value as tools for higher levels of understanding and comprehension of the mysteries of life. Nobility and commoner read them with the idea of using their wisdom in day-to-day life. Some sages employed tales to unlock the doors to human personality traits. It may not be coincidental that the Christian Holy Bible has the format of a storybook. In Qur'an, Islam's Holy Book, God commands, "So relate the Stories; Perchance they may reflect" (VII–176). Without reflection, stories become just another form of entertainment. Furthermore, this pastime was often used to amuse rulers and governors by individuals often referred to as jesters or clowns. They were not taken seriously, so they could often say anything and get away with it. As tyrants came to power and remained in power, certain wise men disguised as jesters took it upon themselves either to remind rulers to pay better attention to the conditions of the society, or to reveal their lack of mercy. In the Middle East the term used to refer to these people was 'wise mad-men'. One of the most important of these 'wise mad-men' was Bahlul; another was the hero of this book, Mulla Nasrudin. (Bahlul lived in the city of Kufa in today's Iraq, and died in the year AD 812. His fame throughout history is due to the fact that such great Sufi masters as Attar and Rumi have relayed tales about him.)

Tales of Mulla Nasrudin were never told by any great Sufi masters but somehow the common man began to identify with him. In fact, no one knows for sure that such a character ever lived. He, however, is so close to people's hearts that no one wants to believe that he did not exist. In Turkey, a tomb is attributed to him stating his death to have been in 1208. Moreover, his supposed birth and death dates are celebrated each year in that country.

As the title *Mulla* implies, Nasrudin was an educated man. This title was given to men who had a mastery of various fields of religious sciences. Interestingly enough, his name Nasrudin may have the meaning of 'victory of religion', which leads to the speculation that this too could have been bestowed upon him for his achievements. It is clear from his anecdotes that he had, indeed, held a position at the pulpit and had taught. Moreover, he had been a consultant and advisor to the local rulers where he lived.

A basic feature of Nasrudin's tales or jokes is his extremely simple character. He constantly puts himself in very awkward situations and tries to get himself out by simple and innocent solutions. The 'punch line' that a westerner expects does not exist; to get the humor, one has to read in between the lines and keep the entire situation in mind.

What has made Mulla Nasrudin and his anecdotes of use to the people of Middle East is, on the one hand, the ease with which they can comprehend and explain human behavior, and on the other hand their ability to convey a level of common sense wisdom which otherwise might be too difficult to bring out in the open. There are even some who might pass on a certain knowledge of human psychology to their followers using a very selected set of these tales.

Westerners will probably have to go through a process of familiarization when it comes to this type of story. It was precisely for that purpose that this work was compiled and is presented here. Generally, the western mind works linearly and very precise deductions are made—a conclusion is only drawn when all the facts have been presented and considered. The Eastern and Middle Eastern mind tends to speculate and draw images of the 'whole' picture—the more facts that are presented, the more complete this picture becomes.

Some of the most obvious examples of this difference were the problems that came up a few decades ago when Americans and Japanese entered into business negotiations. Now that these problems are recognized, many classes are offered to those who might find themselves in similar situations so as to familiarize them with the (then) Japanese and (now) Chinese way of thinking in order to conduct business.

The issue of misunderstanding may now have been resolved to some extent for the businessmen, but how about those interested in the cultures of the East and Middle East, or their mysticism and the tales of the many influential mystics who have lived in those cultures?

In an attempt to reduce the gap between the two cultures, *Tales from the Land of Sufis* [Mojdeh Bayat & Mohammad Ali

Jamnia, 1994, Shambhala Publications] and *Under The Sufi's Cloak; Stories of Abu Said and His Mystical Teaching* [Mohammad Ali Jamnia & Mojdeh Bayat, 1995, Writers Inc. International] were written. Now it is time for the *Tales of Nasrudin* to further educate westerners as to the way an easterner might think and/or react in a given situation. A commentary on each 'joke' is provided so that the underlying wisdom might be brought out. It goes without saying that the commentaries are only our reflections on the Nasrudin tales at this moment of time. The reader might agree or disagree. A few months or a few years from now, we might have a completely different understanding of them. These commentaries are named *keys* to signify that they are there to unlock certain modes of thinking and reflecting.

As it was pointed out earlier, the stories of Nasrudin were kept in the people's hearts and were passed down from generation to generation. When they were first compiled is not at all clear. The Persian copy available to us was put together around the turn of the 20th century and its author is not mentioned. In the past, Idries Shah, Nakosteen and Wilcox each produced collections of these jokes—some of which are similar to the ones we have translated for this collection. What we believe are missing in the other works are the explanations or what we have called 'keys'. It is our hope that, through efforts of this nature, peoples of east and west may come together in a common understanding.

I

THE WISEST OF SAGES

Once Mulla took his sick mother to a doctor who prescribed the cure to be a husband for her. Upon leaving, his mother said, "This man must be the wisest of all sages who knows such a sweet cure!"

KEY

Although short, this story does ask a couple of questions that should be noticed. First, how many people keep going to churches, group therapy, or meditation groups only because they are told something that makes them feel good? The question of what one wants versus what one needs is very old. Second, how many people have managed to get themselves accepted as being wise by simply telling their followers what they want to hear?

And yet, *marriage is half the religion* [*hadith* of Muhammad]. Our deepest desires are implanted in us by God, in order to bring us to Him. Addiction to vice and passion simply means that we have decided to settle for far less than God wants to give us. Knowing ourselves as filled with egotism, we tend to distrust even our true desires—and yet this distrust can be a form of egotism in itself. The wisest of sages is the one who can make us truly objective about who we are and what we really need, thus leading us to 'repent of repentance'. When God is the cure, why accept anything less?

2

THE DONKEY'S SADDLE

One day Mulla was passing by a village. It was the time for ritual prayer so he stopped by a stream, took off his robe and put it over his donkey. Then he began to wash in preparation for the prayers. While he was praying, a thief stole his robe and ran away. Mulla got very angry when he came back and did not see his robe. So, he took the saddle from the donkey and placing it on his back, said to the donkey, "When you give my robe back, I will give you your saddle back!"

KEY

We blame the wrong person or circumstance for our predicaments all the time. Then, we make the situation worse by trying to punish the wrong person (or group). Often such actions are snap decisions made without investigating the situation. This story also illustrated the common occurrence of taking your anger out on someone other than the person (or situation) that caused you to be angry in the first place.

And to misdirect our anger includes misdirecting it against ourselves. When we try to dress our lower self (the donkey) in the honorific robe of the human state—*Have you seen him who makes his desire his god?* [Q. 45:23]—we only take on a donkey's burdens, and lose the robe as well. But to expect the lower self which has stolen our human essence to restore it just because we are willing to bear its burdens for it is doubly foolish. Our only recourse is to saddle the donkey (bridle the lower self) and resume our journey. In the course of this journey, God willing, perhaps we will encounter the thief (Satan, or the World)—this time recognizing him for who he is—and be restored to the human state.

3

HOW MANY TIMES THE FOOL

One day, Mulla took a sack of wheat to the mill. It so happened that the mill-keeper was busy and did not see him. So Mulla began taking wheat from other sacks and adding to his own. The mill-keeper saw what he was doing and shouted, "Why are you doing that?"

"Because, I am a fool," replied Mulla.

"If that is the case, why aren't you pouring your wheat into other sacks?" asked the miller.

"I am once a fool, so I take from others. But if I gave to others, I would be twice a fool!" answered Mulla.

KEY

One usually uses the phrase "I do not know what came over me" (or similar expressions) to justify certain actions for personal gain which are contrary to the society's codes of conduct. However, to go against the society's code of conduct for the benefit of others would generally defy the instinct of self-preservation, and require commitment and dedication.

And to take spiritual teaching promiscuously from anywhere and everywhere is to end up with a 'mixed bag'; the only thing worse would be to try and teach this kind of eclectic or 'polytheistic' doctrine to others—and then have the misfortune to be believed!

4

RIDING THE CAMEL

Once Mulla was riding a camel. He lost control of the animal and the camel took a different road than Nasrudin wanted. On the way, he came across an old friend who asked him, "Where are you going Mulla?"

"I'm going wherever my camel desires!" replied Mulla.

KEY

Have you ever started some small project only to have it slowly (or quickly) take over your life? Work, family, friends all reach out to control our lives. More important, our own thoughts run amuck leading us to see the world as other than what it is.

As a second consideration, it is interesting that in Arabic the word for reasoning, 'Aql, is from the same family of words as 'Eqala, meaning to tie the legs of a steed (e.g. a camel). In other words, reasoning is the human faculty designed to control ego's desires and wants, to prevent it from taking any wrongful actions. In this story, Mulla might have lost control of the camel of his desires. Maybe, he could eventually gain control again!

'Aql is the hobble and bridle of the lower self, without which we will surely go astray. But when God Himself leads the camel from the Unseen, then to follow *'aql* is only disobedience. So how can we tell the difference between the suggestions of the lower self, and God's Command directed *to* the lower self? The Sufi poet Omar Khayyam answers (from his *Rubaiyat*): "Then to the rolling Heaven itself I cried / What lamp had Destiny to guide / Her little children, stumbling in the dark? / 'A blind understanding,' Heaven replied."

5

IN THE MARKET

One day, Mulla took an old robe to the market to sell. No one bought it because they all said that it was torn, had holes, and was worthless.

Mulla disagreed. "That is a lie. If it had holes, my mother would not store cotton balls in it."

KEY

In a round about way, this story shows how we will cling to our beliefs even when it becomes obvious they are wrong. A child's problems in school are not dismissed by his excellence on the football field nor is a lover's infidelity excused by their ability to cook a good meal. So too, the cotton-holding capacity of Nasrudin's robe has nothing to do with how useful it is as a piece of clothing.

6

GETTING OLD

Once, while in a group of people, Mulla exclaimed, "even though I am now old, my strength has not changed from the time I was young." Everyone marveled at this and wondered how Mulla knew what he said was true.

"I know this," said Mulla, "because there is a small stone in my house that I could not move when I was young. Now that I am old, I still can not move it! So, the only conclusion is that my strength has not changed."

KEY

The idea of measuring one's progress is sometimes a good idea. In school, in business, even in a relationship, the constant flux can be given meaning by seeing if it has a direction and what that direction is. However, one has to be selective about how they go about measuring progress and more important, what they measure against. You may want to keep up with the Jones's, but if the Jones's abilities or resources are so far above (or beneath) your own, it's a meaningless comparison. There is an old saying that one should judge the outcome of something by the original intention. If one meant to build a doghouse but ends up with something the size of a condominium, perhaps they have overshot their original intention.

Time does not automatically confer spiritual capacity. Our body may grow, mature, age, and decay according to its own laws, but not so our Spirit. Those who falsely identify spiritual capacity with physical or psychic vitality will lose all they have seemed to gain, like a mirror turned momentarily toward the sun, then away from it again. Growth in the Spirit may *use* time, but it does not happen *in* time.

7

GOING TO A GATHERING

A group of rich people built a garden for their pleasure. One spring day, they had a party and invited Nasrudin to entertain them. The garden had an auditorium centered in it so that any breeze would bring the scent of the flowers. Two of the four walls had eight doors each and the other two had five doors for a total of twenty-eight doors. As a joke, someone asked "Mulla, which season is this hall best for?"

Nasrudin replied, "For winter of course. I live in a room with only one door and when I close it, so much heat enters that I have no need for a heater. Now, if so much heat is generated by one door, just think what twenty-eight doors would do."

KEY

This story is difficult to understand even for people who are from Nasrudin's homeland. Still, if we remember a couple of key points, it makes sense. First, Mulla Nasrudin lives in a land where the accepted religion is Islam. Second, Islam uses a lunar calendar. Third, the lunar calendar has twenty-eight days per month. So what Nasrudin is doing here is making a covert reference to Islam. In other words, his strict monotheism gives him great satisfaction (warmth). Now, if his monotheism takes the form of Islam, he will receive twenty-eight times the warmth. It should be noted that the idea of paradise (i.e. heaven) as a garden is a Persian idea.

If one opens a door in winter, cold enters. Does this mean that if one closes the door, then heat will enter? Where could it possibly come from? From the Unseen Realm. The fire of the Spirit can only grow when our inner room is sealed against the world, when the lower self can no longer steal fire from the Secret. So one's heart must go cold to the world. This is relatively easy when we are in the realm of the Unity of God, where the world does not encroach upon His Incomparability.[1] But if we can close the other twenty-seven doors in the midst of outer conditions, then we will know God in the secret of his Comparability too;[2] we will meet Him in all the conditions of life, not just during a forty-day retreat or the like. The Prophet Muhammad, peace and blessings be upon him, was both a contemplative and a man of action; he took heat from the closing of all twenty-eight doors. This is why the moon is his appropriate symbol.

---

1. *Tanzih*, Transcendence. When the Qur'an, in the *surah At-Tauhid*, says: "He neither begets nor is begotten, and there is nothing to which He can be compared," it is asserting God's Incomparability.

2. *Tashbih*, Immanence. When the *surah Fatihah*, calls God "Lord of the

8

MULLA'S SERMON

Once a group of people asked Nasrudin to go to the pulpit and give a sermon. Mulla climbed up to the pulpit and addressed the crowd.

"O people, praise the Lord that camels do not have wings like the birds of the air. Just think if camels did have wings, they would land on your roofs and destroy them!"

KEY

In a funny way, Nasrudin is referring to the order that God has given to the world. Why don't camels have wings? Because God didn't make them that way! Besides, if camels had wings, it will be almost impossible to catch them and make them serve as pack animals for the caravan. After all, what animal in its right mind would want to carry hundreds of pounds of cargo across blazing deserts?

Or, more briefly: Don't try to spiritualize the lower self! And if you do, recognize your ultimate failure as God's Mercy.

Worlds, Owner of the Day of Judgment," it is asserting God's Comparability. If He were totally unlike anything we know, we could never know Him; also, there would be no universe. The universe does not exist *in addition* to God, as if it were a second God, but 'exists' *by analogy* to Him; it is composed only of symbols of His Reality and signs of His Presence. It is interesting that the word for 'signs', *ayat*, is also used for the verses of the Qur'an.

9

GOD'S ANGELS

Nasrudin was asked, "Mulla, before God created the universe, where did the angels live?"

"In God's house."

KEY

This story is similar to the answer to the question, "What was God doing before he made the world?" The quick answer is that he was making hell for all who ask such questions. Often the way one formulates a question determines the type of answer they will get. If a question is asked that obviously can't be answered, perhaps the question is meaningless.

On the other hand, the simplest answer may be the truest and deepest one. A house that is not created can only belong to God, and as Ibn al-'Arabi taught, the 'permanent archetypes' of all created things were with God in pre-eternity, before the Breath of the Merciful gave them separate existence.

And they are even now as they were.[1]

1. This phrase is in reference to an exchange that happened between the Prophet Muhammad and his son-in-law Ali ibn Abi Talib, who was later to become both the Fourth Caliph and the first of the Twelve Imams of the Shi'ites. The Prophet said, "Before the creation God was alone, without a partner," to which Ali replied: "And He is even now as He was."

10

DIFFERENCES

Nasrudin was asked, "What is the number of differences among the people?"

"As many as the number of Adam's children. I know that number very well."

"Really? And what is that number?"

"Well," Nasrudin hesitated, "My memory fails me on the number of sons and the number of daughters I have forgotten."

KEY

Past a certain point it makes little sense to analytically think about something. How big is infinity? At what point does a number become so big that it doesn't really matter if it's infinite or not (because the human mind can no longer think about it in concrete terms)?

The number is One—or infinity. Each created form is unique since it is a reflection of God's Uniqueness, but once things are divided into sons and daughters, into pairs of opposites, we have already lost count. In the loins of Adam, all the future generations were as one. [cf. Q. 7:189] And they are even now as they were.

11

STARS IN THE SKY

Mulla was asked, "Do you know the number of stars in the sky?"

"I have pondered this question," replied Nasrudin, "and looked for the answer. In fact, the only way I could find out for certain would be to climb up to the heavens and count them myself. But there are two obstacles that I have not been able to resolve. First, I can not undertake this task during the day because with work and the hassles of living, I don't have enough time. Second, if I should do this job at night, I am afraid there would not be enough light in the sky and as you know, it is very difficult to count anything in the dark."

KEY

This story is very similar to the last. The number of stars is so large, one could spend a life time counting and never reach the end. There are some things that one can think about and do only after the right preparation. There are other things one could do but the real question should be, are they worth all the time and effort? After all, how important is it to count the 1000000001^{st} star when we have to busy ourselves making a living and supporting a family?

Involved in conditions, we lose the serenity and objectivity necessary to understand them. Detached from conditions, they disappear. If we can't understand them by either finding them or losing them, were they ever really there?

12

THE MULLA'S STATEMENT

Once Nasrudin went to the pulpit and said, "O people, know that the atmosphere in my town is very similar to yours."

The audience wondered how Nasrudin knew this. "Because, I have noticed that you have the same constellations over your town that are over mine."

KEY

This story captures the relativity of cultural and religious beliefs in a nutshell. It may be true that on some absolute level that all religions aim at the same ends but no one is ever going to step completely outside their own knowledge and experiences. So perhaps the stars (the ultimate objects of human beliefs) are the same but the idea that the villages are the same (like saying that religions are the same) hardly follows.

Or, this tale may bring out the tendency to make judgments based on superficial evidence. Rumi has a beautiful narration of a dialog between a bald parrot and a bald Sufi and the parrot's assumption that he and the Sufi are really equals on the basis of their baldness. This story is retold in *Tales from the Land of the Sufis.*

13

WATCHING THE DOOR

One day, Nasrudin's mother went to a gathering and told Mulla to watch the door. Nasrudin sat by the door waiting but his mother did not return. He became bored. So he took the door off the hinges, put in on his back and went off to the market with his friends.

KEY

Well, she didn't say where he had to watch the door. Language, when taken out of context, can make communication difficult. Since we don't always know all the conditions that an event took place under, perhaps it's best not to jump to conclusions too quickly. What we are hearing may not be the entire story just like simply watching the door (so no one could come into the house to steal) involves more that just the door.

An early woman Sufi, Rabi'a, called herself a 'doorkeeper of the heart'. We are told to become doorkeepers so as to protect the Heart from being darkened by unconscious impressions streaming in from the outer world. But when vigilance becomes willful and obsessive, then the act of vigilance itself is transformed into an open doorway to unconscious impressions. So we need to realize that our true vigilance ultimately comes from somewhere beyond us. *Pray to God as if you saw Him, because even if you don't see Him, He sees you* [*hadith* of Muhammad].

14

THE FREE HAIRCUT

Once, Nasrudin and a young boy entered a barber shop together. As they came in, Mulla told the barber that he was in a hurry and so wanted to get his hair cut before the boy. Agreeably, the barber cut his hair first. Nasrudin checked his hair, took his turban, said he would be back soon and left. The barber gave the boy a hair cut and afterward, waited. Nasrudin was nowhere to be found.

"Your father is late," said the barber.

"Father? He is not my father! He is a man I met on the street who told me to come along for a free hair cut!"

KEY

Nasrudin can sometimes be a rascal. Yet, we often let our own assumptions of what other people are doing make us like the barber. Con men are professionals at taking advantage of people's assumptions. Maybe the barber should have asked the boy or Nasrudin who was who. It would have saved him some time, not to mention giving away a hair cut. If you think back, you too may find examples in your own life where you have ended up like the barber.

15

NASRUDIN AND THE MAID

Once Nasrudin saw his father's maid sleeping. He curled up next to her. She awoke with a fright, "Who are you?" she exclaimed.

"I am my father!" Replied Mulla.

KEY

Dressing like someone else, acting like someone or even claiming to be someone whom you are not does not change the fact that you are who you are. No amount of acting will allow you the privileges and rights earned by someone else.

16

NASRUDIN'S VOICE

One day, Mulla went to a public bathhouse, which happened to be empty. Calling out to see if anyone was around, he heard the echo of his own voice. He liked the sound so much, he began to sing to himself. He enjoyed it so much that he decided to share his 'beautiful' voice with everyone. So he left the bath for the first minaret. Climbing to the top, he began singing at the top of his lungs. Someone passed by and yelled up that he should not torture everyone with his voice. Nasrudin was ashamed and climbed down. As he headed home, he told himself, "What a shame that no one had built a bath house on top of a minaret so I could sing for the world to enjoy!"

KEY

Beauty (as art) is in the eye of the beholder. Of course, it is much easier to hold one's own art in higher esteem than it deserves. It also easier to come up with excuses when everyone doesn't see the same merit in our work as we do.

God sees and speaks only to Himself, and to all other things only as aspects of Himself. With us it is different; when we see and speak only to ourselves, this is called 'narcissism'. What is beautiful in the intimacy of the inner Heart is only vulgar and tasteless when broadcast to the world. Yet the job of the muezzin is to reveal what is inner outwardly, so that what is outer can turn back and journey toward what is inner: *Come to prayer; come to salvation.*[1] Rumi said: "When I came to love, I became ashamed of everything I had ever said about love." If one dares to speak about love openly, one must be careful to be overheard speaking only to one's Beloved. Yes, there are many minarets that would be greatly improved by being crowned with bath houses.

1. These words are part of the *adhan*, the Muslim call to prayer sounded by the *muezzin*.

17

THE BLOWING WIND

Nasrudin took a basket and went to a farm to collect some turnips and prunes. The owner came out and shouted, "What are you doing here? What's in your basket?"

"The wind blew me here," answered Nasrudin.

"Okay, if the wind blew you here," said the farmer "then who has picked these prunes and turnips?"

Mulla answered, "If the wind is strong enough to blow a man away, he would surely try to grab anything near by to save himself."

"Maybe that is the case," said the owner, "but who has put everything in your basket?"

"You know, I was just pondering that when you arrived," replied Nasrudin.

KEY

This wouldn't be an ancient form of the insanity plea would it? Getting oneself into trouble by one's own decisions and then claiming to be victim of outside forces is a very, very old human habit.

The wind of the Spirit of God moves us along all the paths of life. If we were to let ourselves be blown wherever He wished, we would not accumulate all the baggage that weighs us down. Even God's gifts are a kind of baggage. If we resist His will, we may end up holding His gifts—rather earthly gifts, at that—instead of flying with Him to the ends of the earth.

18

CRACKING NUTS

Mulla was cracking some walnuts when one slipped from his hands and disappeared. He exclaimed, "Hallelujah, everything tries to escape death—even the ones who are not yet born."

KEY

People give pointless attributes to things all the time. We talk about our troubles as if they have a life all their own and they are somehow choosing to victimize us through their own design. So too, some blame their cars, houses and compact disc players for breaking down when maybe they should place the blame on the maker (or their own lack of attention to maintenance). So, don't give objects more credit (for intention) than they really deserve.

In a sense, to be born is to die and to die is to be born. And so to resist death is really no different from not even wanting to be born in the first place. But to *die before you are made to die* [*hadith* of Muhammad] is to become all nourishment.

19

MURDERED MAN OR RAM

One morning, Nasrudin was about to leave his house when he saw the corpse of a man who had been murdered. He picked the body up and threw it in the well in his garden. Then he left. Mulla's son was awake and saw the whole event. The son came out, took the man's body from the well and then killed a ram and dropped it in the well. Afterward, he hid the body.

Meanwhile, the victim's family came across Nasrudin and asked him if he had seen their relative. Nasrudin said he had and told them where the body was. They all went back to the well and lowered Mulla down on a rope so he could pull the body out. When Nasrudin touched the body, he felt the ram's horns, so he asked, "Does your dead have any horns?"

KEY

This story shows one possible way to react to a very unexpected event. Instead of jumping up and down and repeatedly telling the relatives that their missing body was not where it is supposed to be, Nasrudin simply states the facts and lets them make of it what they can (or will).

The Mulla probably hid the corpse in his own well to escape being charged with murder—not a very good hiding-place if one wishes to avoid the appearance of guilt. Nasrudin's son apparently thought that his father actually was the murderer, so he hid the body elsewhere and put a slaughtered ram in its place, undoubtedly to explain where all the blood came from.

There is nothing that can make us seem guiltier than the act of denying guilt; even though Nasrudin was innocent of the man's blood, his attempt to hide the crime nonetheless involved him in it. Nasrudin's son may symbolize his spiritual essence, especially in view of the fact that in traditional Arabic names, someone who is known for a particular quality is often named "Father [*Abu*] of [such-and-such a quality]." The hidden corpse may represent an unconscious sin—the great majority of our sins are probably unconscious—which Nasrudin's son has made atonement for by slaughtering the ram. And since Nasrudin is now free of unconscious guilt, while never having incurred any conscious guilt, this innocence—in the guise of foolishness—now leads him to say the very thing that will convinced everyone that he could not possibly be the murderer. To hide a public danger is to incur guilt, but to hide the personal sin of another is sometimes an expression of true piety, which is one reason why Muslims often say "may God keep his secret."

20

GETTING SICK

When Nasrudin got sick, a group of relatives went to visit him. They stayed so long and ate so much that their welcome wore off. Eventually, Nasrudin got out of his bed and exclaimed, "God has healed your sick relative. You can go home now!"

KEY

In the Middle East, one is supposed to visit one's sick relatives as a religious obligation. Some explain this by the fact that by seeing the loved-ones, the sick person might be gladdened and the joy would help the recovery. But this visitation should not be overdone, as it will be a burden on the host family. It might therefore be realized here that good deeds not only depend on the actions of the one giving but also on the conditions and the capacity of the one receiving.

If we identify with too many things, persons and situations, giving each one some of our life-energy, we will become ill—spiritually, and perhaps even physically. Do we want people to pity us because we are sick, or is it their pity that is making us sick in the first place? To identify with the world around us is to try and incorporate it, to swallow it whole. But the world always swallows us instead, like the whale swallowed the Prophet Yunnus [Jonah]. Send away the 'cure', and the disease will leave along with it. When God heals us, then we can dismiss the world.

21

MULLA'S SERMON

One day, Nasrudin went to the pulpit and asked, "O people, do you know what I want to talk about?"

"Yes, we do, Mulla," replied the crowd.

"So, repeating it is a futile task." Saying this, Nasrudin left.

The following day, he went back to the same pulpit and asked the same question. This time though, the crowd claimed no knowledge. To everyone's surprise, Mulla proclaimed, "Well, I can not give words of wisdom to those who don't know!" He straightened his turban and left.

On the third day, the audience was poised and ready. When Nasrudin asked the same question, some said they knew and some said they did not. To this Nasrudin declared, "Well, let those who know tell those who don't." Then he left.

KEY

Have you ever noticed how people let the source of information color their view as to whether the information is true or not? Let your next door neighbor (who you have known for years) start explaining something to you and you will almost immediately turn them off. Let a teacher start telling the exact same thing and you will accept it as if the information took on something special just because of who gave it to you. While it may be true that in some instances that one needs to get their information from an authority, that rarely changes the basic quality of that information.

Furthermore, if you think you already know something you will never learn it, just as knowledge will never become truly your own if you see yourself as inherently ignorant, only fit to be filled—still in ignorance—with the knowledge of someone else. If you really want to learn, the humility to admit your ignorance and the readiness to make knowledge truly your own must come together.

This is a story about what Plato called *anamnesis*, 'remembering'. According to Plato, we know everything already, but have forgotten that we know it; the purpose of *education*, which means 'leading out', is to help the part of us that already knows to teach the part of us that doesn't. Likewise, in Sufi practice, *ghaflah*, 'heedlessness', is overcome by *dhikr*, 'remembering'. Prophet Muhammad made it clear that he did not come to teach anything new; his only role was to help the people remember.

22

MULLA'S DREAM

One night, Nasrudin dreamt that someone was giving him nine gold pieces. So he decided to bargain and asked for ten pieces. Suddenly, he woke up and found that he had no gold. Immediately he closed his eyes and, extending his hand, said, "Okay, I'll take the nine pieces."

KEY

How many of us have lost something valuable because we were busy chasing something else that simply was not there. More than a few relationships end because of this. Before passing by something you already have for something that is only a dream, perhaps you should ask if in fact what you want is even there at all.

Or if *what you think you already have* is really there at all.

23

IN THE GRAVE

One day Nasrudin was passing through a graveyard situated outside the city. Suddenly, he saw three riders coming. Fearing for his life, he took his cloths off and hid himself in a nearby open grave.

The riders noticed Nasrudin moving about and came over to ask who he was. "I'm one of the dead but I noticed the good weather and decided to come out for a walk."

KEY

This story could be taken as a reference to how some people go to extreme ends to present a situation as other than it is. No one returns to life (at least in the same body) and yet our Mulla uses this absurd excuse to protect himself and his interests from people he considers (without proof) his enemies.

He who sees the signs of death approaching—danger, sickness, old age—should not automatically grab for more life. Instead, he should flee *from* death *to* death; he should *die before he is made to die.* If he can really do this, then he will be resurrected into eternal life—where the weather is always pleasant—and death will have no power over him. *There is no refuge from God, but in Him.* [Q. 9:118]

24

MULLA AND THE *HALWA*

Once, Mulla was in a *halwa* pastry shop. He began eating from the *halwa* trays on the counter without bothering to ask the owner. The shopkeeper realized that if he wasted a moment, there wouldn't be a trace of *halwa* left in his shop. He snatched up a stick and began hitting Nasrudin.

Ignoring the beating, Nasrudin kept on eating but at the same time, he began giving praise. "God bless the people of this city who force sweet *halwa* on others with a beating!"

KEY

This strange account says more than that some *halwa* is worth a beating. In Sufism and some forms of Christian mysticism, the mystics do not perfect themselves by denying themselves but rather by developing love. The idea is as simple as it is profound. If one uses strict self-discipline, there is always the chance that one will backslide. However, just as love can make a person loyal to their beloved (in spite of temptations), so too, love can be used in the place of discipline to develop a person. The idea is that the more one loves (in this case, *halwa*), the less burdensome (here, a beating) the difficulties of life are, because, by its nature, love lessens all burdens.

On the other hand, those who love truly will be willing to endure great sufferings for the sake of that love. As soon as love dawns, everything in our soul or in the world that hates love will dawn at the same time. To endure the blows of hatred for the sake of love is perhaps the greatest way of deepening love and purifying it, but any 'love' that shows no willingness to suffer is not even worth the name. Asceticism without love is mere suffering for the sake of the ego; asceticism in the name of love is both true asceticism and true love, each being the cause and proof of the other.

One day Rabi'a was discussing with two other Sufis how to recognize the perfection of Islam. "It is to resign oneself to God's chastisement," said the first. "It is to rejoice in God's chastisement," said the second. "Not bad," said Rabi'a, "but I know something better: It is not even to recognize that any chastisement has occurred."

25

TRACKING THE DAYS OF RAMADAN

One year, near the month of Ramadan, Nasrudin decided to devise a method for keeping track of the number of days which had passed in the month. He figured that if he put twenty-eight date pits beside a jar and every day he put one pit in the jar, he could know the number of days passed by simply counting the pits. When all the pits outside the jar were in the jar, Ramadan would be over.

The Mulla's daughter found out what her father was doing and, deciding to have a little fun, she put a handful of pits inside the jar.

Several days later, some of Nasrudin's friends were visiting.

When the conversation came around to the number of days that had passed in Ramadan, no one could agree. Nasrudin asked the group to wait as he had access to the correct answer. He went to his jar and counted the pits. He found the number to be one hundred and twenty. He thought if he announced that number, no one would believe him so he decided to use a third of that number.

He went back to his friends and announced, "The number of days that have passed in the month of Ramadan is forty."

"But how can that be Mulla?" Replied the group. "There are only twenty-eight days in a month."

"I know! It really is my fault for not being truthful." Replied Mulla. "For in fact, one hundred and twenty days of Ramadan have passed!"

KEY

Sometimes, if you want to borrow money, you ask for twice the amount you really want. That way, if you get half of what you ask for, you end up where you wanted. When breaking unbelievable news, sometimes you start small and work your way up. On another level, this story shows how dogmatic anyone can be. If your evidence is so completely removed from all possibilities, perhaps you need to question the evidence. In everyday life, common sense is often an overlooked resource.

And who ate all those dates in the first place? Our sweet, hungry little soul is liable to gobble up our entire fast, while maintaining (with great humility) that we are over four times as self-denying as everybody else. She will become fat on the meat while we break our teeth on the pits, and life will soon have run out, before we even know it.

26

ENJOYING THE COMPANY OF WOMEN

The King enjoyed spending an excessive amount of time and money on women. Nasrudin repeatedly told him to curb his appetite for the fairer sex. Eventually, the ruler began to listen and ignored his consorts. One of them, a beautiful slave, was surprised by the ruler's lack of attention and wondered why she had fallen out of favor. Upon hearing of the ruler's decision to heed Nasrudin's advice, she said, "Give me to the Mulla as a present. I will teach him a lesson he will not forget."

From the first day she came to live in his house, Nasrudin took an interest in her. Every time they were alone, he wanted to have his way with her but she always refused. Eventually, she set a condition for their union. "If you are truthful to me then let me ride on your back. That way, I will know the extent of your desire for me."

Nasrudin found this to be an easy condition. He offered his back to her but this was not what she had in mind. "Oh no. It is not proper for a lady to ride without a saddle." So Nasrudin shrugged and went to the barn to put a saddle on his back. Again he presented himself. "Oh, no. It is not proper for a lady to ride unless her mount has a bridle in his mouth." So Nasrudin went back to the barn. While he was putting on his bridle, the slave girl motioned to one of the house servant who scampered off.

When Nasrudin returned, the slave girl climbed up onto the saddle and began riding. A minute or two into the ride, the King came riding up. "What has come over you Mulla? You advise me to control myself around women and look at how you have become enslaved yourself."

Nasrudin kept prancing around the yard with the slave girl on his back. "Me? Why, not at all! My advice to you was for times like this. See, I didn't want them to make a jack-ass out of you like they have done to me."

KEY

At face value, this story contains several lessons. Not the least of which is: be careful how you say someone else should live if you can't live up to what you are saying. In the case of men and women, few really live up to what they believe and that applies to Mulla as well as everyone else.

Furthermore, it is for the asinine lower self to be ridden by lust, not for the King, the Spirit. When lust no longer blinds the Spirit's eyes, the unlovely truth of it can be seen for what it is, rather than its being mistaken for some kind of spiritual state. Until we become object-lessons to ourselves, some of us will never learn.

27

PURCHASING A DONKEY

One day, Mulla took some money and went to the market to buy a donkey. On the way, he came across a friend who asked him what he was doing.

"I'm going to the market to buy a donkey."

The friend shook his head. "You should say 'God willing'."

Nasrudin shrugged. "There is no need. The market has the donkey and I have the money in my pocket. Of course I will buy the donkey."

A short while later, after the two friends had separated, a group of bandits surrounded Nasrudin and robbed him.

On his way back home, a disappointed Nasrudin came across the same friend. "Mulla, where is your donkey?"

Nasrudin glared at his friend. "The money was stolen! God willing, God would smash your mouth. God willing indeed!"

KEY

There's a time and a place for everything. Prayers for a safe journey should be made before the journey. Getting angry at someone who has pointed this out to you won't do you a bit of good either.

And sometimes God withholds us from a particular sin by His own choice, whether we want Him to or not, proving that what we consider to be our goodness is drawn entirely from the store of His goodness. And getting angry at Him for this great show of Mercy won't do you a bit of good.

28

GIVING A PARTY

Nasrudin had a lamb he had spent months fattening. His friends wanted to trick him into slaughtering it for them. One day, they came to him and said, "Tomorrow may be the day of Resurrection and Judgment. Let's go to a nice place, slaughter the lamb and enjoy ourselves today."

Mulla agreed. Everyone went down to the river. After lunch, the weather turned hot and everyone decided to go for a swim. Everyone except Nasrudin stripped and jumped into the cool river. Once his friends were in the water, Nasrudin gathered up their clothes and burned everything. Running and sputtering from the river, they all demanded an explanation. "Well my friends, you said tomorrow is the Day of Resurrection. If that's so, then there will be no need for clothing."

KEY

Of course, the lamb was going to be slaughtered eventually— so why not let the meat be shared with friends and have a good time in the process? It is always possible that tomorrow is the Day of Resurrection, but being somewhat wise, Nasrudin saw no reason to bet everything on his friends' claims. He only agreed to enjoy what everyone else claimed to be the last day. However, he did not burn his own clothes. His friends may have enjoyed the lamb and their joke on Nasrudin but it is doubtful that they enjoyed the consequences of their own actions (walking home naked, especially since Nasrudin was simply doing what was logically congruent to their story).

Nasrudin's friends invoked the Day of Judgment and Resurrection, but did not want to remember that this Day will strip of us of both our earthly bodies and any lamb those bodies could feast upon. They wanted to bathe in the rivers of Paradise only in order to forget Paradise's inescapable twin, the Fire. It is better to keep one's earthly clothes and earthly lamb, as Nasrudin did, than to falsely attempt to transcend this world through mere imagination, taking Paradise to be no more than a picnic on a summer day. Paradise is God's Beauty, but it is not without its own Rigor and Majesty. According to one contemporary Sufi,[1] the Rigor of Paradise is based on the grave responsibility of the dwellers of Paradise to *be* Paradise for one another.

---

1. Abu Bakr Siraj al-Din, whose English name was Martin Lings.

29

WEIGHING THE CAT

One day, Nasrudin bought six ponds of meat and asked his wife to cook a nice dish with it. Then he left to run an errand. His wife did so, but a friend came by and the two of them ate everything. When Nasrudin came home and asked about the food, his wife exclaimed, "The cat ate the meat when I wasn't looking!"

Suspicious, Nasrudin picked the cat up and put her on a scale. The cat weighed six pounds. Shaking his head knowingly, Nasrudin asked, "Here is six pounds for the meat. Now, what happened to the *cat's* weight?"

KEY

There is some danger in being too clever. Someone might get around to simply checking the very facts you created your story with.

Also, like the cat, we become what we eat, till finally there is nothing of us left. This is what happens to people—like Nasrudin's wife and her friend—who are greedy for experience: they become totally determined by what has happened to them, and lose themselves in the process.

30

GOING TO THE BATHHOUSE

One day, Nasrudin asked his wife to prepare some soup for him. Then he left and went to the bathhouse. While he was gone, his wife took the food to some friends, and together they finished the entire pot. When Nasrudin returned, he asked for the soup. Claiming that it wasn't finished, Nasrudin's wife suggested that he take a nap. Nasrudin felt tired after his bath so he flopped on the bed and was soon fast asleep. While he slept, his wife covered his beard and mustache with what little was left of the soup. When he awoke, Mulla asked for the soup again.

"Soup?" His wife demanded. "Why you ate all the soup before you went to sleep!"

"What are you talking about?" Nasrudin raised his voice to match his wife's. "I've been sleeping while you were supposed to finish cooking."

"Nasrudin, what has gotten into you? Just check your own beard. It is still covered with soup!"

"What?" Nasrudin checked his beard and apologized profusely.

KEY

There may be two ways of looking at this tale. First, this is a humorous illustration of what happens in a lot of so-called spiritual work. Putting on strange clothes, assuming new names, or adapting strange diets does not make up for total lack of spiritual nutrition. Often, people will confuse the most basic traces of spiritual experience with the total experience just as Nasrudin has confused soup on the beard with soup in the stomach.

Second, a less subtle interpretation is that often one can be mislead by superficial indications. Surely, the soup on the beard may convince anyone that our Mulla has had his share, but with a growling stomach, how can *he* be convinced that he ate the soup? Because he himself is only looking at the outward appearances of things. Having no other evidence, he has no other choice but to accept the 'facts'.

31

A LOVE AFFAIR

One day, Nasrudin came home and found his wife in bed with a stranger. He grabbed the man, tied him up and threw him into a trunk. Then he left to get his wife's relatives to shame her publicly. Meanwhile, his wife opened the trunk and let her lover go. In his place, she pushed a baby donkey into the trunk.

Upon returning with his in-laws, Nasrudin threw open the trunk and the little donkey jumped out and ran away. Enraged at his accusations, his in-laws proceeded to beat the living daylights out of Nasrudin, who was so distracted by his wife's miraculous powers, he couldn't run or fight back.

KEY

Often people think that if they ignore a problem, it will go away. Sometimes it does. Sometimes it just gets worst. Then again, sometimes it does something you could not anticipate and in the process, makes you look like a complete idiot.

And one of the most powerful forms of magic is our ability to belittle our transgressions, both in our own eyes and those of others.

32

THE MADMAN AND THE MULLA

Once upon a time, Mulla Nasrudin came across a madman who pulled out a sword and yelled, "It has been a long time since I made my oath to kill a Mulla."

Instantly, Nasrudin fell to the ground proclaiming, "I swear on all the sacred books and spirits of the saints that I cannot even read, much less be a Mulla!"

KEY

Many people make great claims in regards to who they are and what they believe. Unfortunately, many do not have the conviction to help carry them through tough times. This is not only true on any spiritual path but also for any ideal. Many who aspire to high ideals are often only too eager to let go of their beliefs in order to dispel any trouble or calamity.

Here Nasrudin may claim that he is not a Mulla, but how does he explain his clothing which caused the madman to recognize him in the first place?

The madman swore he would kill a Mulla, and Mulla Nasrudin obliged him by killing off the 'Mulla' in himself. The same thing happened to al-Ghazzali when he joined the Sufis, or to Rumi when he met his master Shams Tabrizi. The madman represents a kind of knowledge that is beyond reason, and so confounds it. Such 'madness' is really a higher sanity sent by God—and if we try to resist it by asserting our known, everyday, 'literal' identity, then we will become mad. Literally. Nasrudin shows that it's much better to become 'unlettered' like Prophet Muhammad.[1]

33

MULLA AND THE EGGPLANTS

It has been told that one day Nasrudin's wife was sitting with her lover when the Mulla came home. He had thirty egg-

---

1. In Q. 7:157 the Prophet Muhammad is called 'unlettered'. In an outer sense, this simply means that he was illiterate—though he undoubtedly had the powerful and well-stocked memory common to nomadic and semi-nomadic peoples. But in an inner sense, to be 'unlettered' means that one's heart is not 'written over' with many impressions and attachments, but stands like a blank sheet of paper, ready to receive the Word of God.

plants that he had just bought in the market. His wife managed to hide her lover in the pantry and came out to greet her husband. Nasrudin gave her the eggplants. She took all but one of them to the pantry. The one eggplant she carefully hid. Screaming, she ran back to Nasrudin crying that one of the eggplants had turned into a man. She screamed that the eggplant seller must have been a magician. Suspicious, Nasrudin went to the pantry and counted the eggplants and found only twenty-nine.

Convinced, he grabbed the man and dragged him back to the market. Confronting the eggplant seller, Nasrudin demanded to know why he was given a man instead of the eggplant he wanted. The seller, being quick witted, realized what had happened and he pulled the man aside, slapped him and shouted, "I have told you a thousand times, you belong to the turnips. Now, don't mix with the eggplants again!" Then he gave Nasrudin another eggplant and sent him home happy.

KEY

There is nothing like creating an artificial crisis to distract someone's attention from the real situation. Incidentally, the emotions associated with a seeker's search can be the very things that keep the seeker from finding what they are looking for (even if it is right in front of them).

(And if you are committed to denying the reality of what you know, the whole world will rush to support you, hoping you will some day return the favor.)

34

THE MULLA'S FATHER

One day, Nasrudin's father asked him to bring him the lunch tray and then close the door. But Nasrudin refused, saying, "No, I shall close the door first and then I bring the tray!" His father exclaimed, "Wow, you are much wiser than I."

KEY

One simple trick for appearing wise is to say things out of their normal order. Furthermore, it would take a powerful wisdom to be able to carry a lunch tray straight through a closed door. The best service is performed in simplicity. How often do we create difficulties for ourselves so that we can appear heroic by overcoming them? How often do we propound unnecessary riddles so that we can appear wise to ourselves by solving them? True seriousness always takes the easiest way, because it is committed to accomplishing the task.

35

PRAISING GOD'S GRACE

One day, a friend brought an entire cooked lamb to Nasrudin's house so everyone could join in a feast. When the meal was finished, someone asked the Mulla to say a prayer for the friend who brought the lamb. Standing before everyone Nasrudin intoned, "May God provide you with lamb's heads from Heaven." Then he sat back down.

KEY

Saying the grace at meal time is very different in the East—particularly in Persia—than the Christian West. Generally, each individual says quietly, "In God's name" and begins his / her meal. Once the meal is finished, a quiet thanksgiving is uttered. If there are any guests present, they provide a short prayer asking God to make sure that the host's table is always full with a variety of foods—a sign of prosperity.

The irony in this story is that Mulla could ask for more—a lot more—but he does not. This reflects his lack of aspirations. We find many people today who have all the tools and opportunities for getting ahead in life and "make something of themselves," but choose inaction and are thus swept away by life's forces.

And if one seriously believes that heaven has the power to grant gifts, it is a kind of niggardliness not to open oneself to heaven's abundance; there can be a lack of generosity—not to mention a lack of imagination!—in the inability to receive, just as much as in the unwillingness to give. But of course the Mulla's stomach was filled with roast lamb, and most likely this seriously diminished his receptive abilities. It is *because* "we are the poor" that, to us, "God is the Rich." [Q. 47:38]

36

THE BROILED LAMB'S HEAD

A common food in Mulla Nasrudin's day was broiled lamb's head which people ate with sugar. One day, Nasrudin's father gave him some money and asked him to go buy a broiled lamb's head. Mulla did as asked but on the way back, he became hungry and proceeded to eat everything. By the time he presented the lamb's head to his father, it was nothing more than bones.

His surprised father exclaimed, "This is bare bones. What happened to its ears?"

"The poor lamb was deaf!" shrugged Nasrudin.

"What happened to its eyes?" asked the father.

"The poor lamb was blind!"

"Well, what about its tongue?"

"Oh father, the lamb was mute too."

"What about the skin on its head?"

"Father, this poor lamb was even bald. But look! It had very strong teeth."

KEY

On the one hand, this story demonstrates that Mulla is just not willing to take the responsibility for his own actions. Clearly, his father knows what has happened and Mulla knows that he knows. However, admitting to what had happened would require Mulla's admission of wrongdoing.

On the other hand, this story demonstrates what happens to some schools of thought over time. As the real value (sometimes called nutrition by certain Mystics) is consumed, all that is left are empty symbols, rituals that belong to a different time and place, and mindless repetition of dogma that no longer applies.

Those who steal nourishment, including spiritual nourishment, have proved that they are unable to receive it, and usually end by devouring themselves, after first becoming deaf, blind and speechless. Still, they do have very good teeth.

37

EATING DUCK

One day, Nasrudin was eating a cooked duck when someone came by and asked for some.

The Mulla replied, "Please pardon me as this was given to me by my wife and it is not mine. I do not have her permission to share it with you."

KEY

On one hand, this story makes more sense if one remembers that the duck is an animal that can live on land, water, or in the air. In much the same way, true transmission (grace or *baraka*) functions in whatever situation it enters. Often one can not share a blessing without the aid (or permission) of its source.

On the other hand, Mulla likes food and he does not care to share. This ridiculous excuse only reveals his greed.

38

EATING DATES

Once a man saw Mulla Nasrudin eating some dates. As he watched, he noticed that Nasrudin was eating both the fruit and the pits. Wondering why, he walked over and asked.

"You see," replied Nasrudin, "the seller sold me the pits along with the dates. Since I have paid for them, I can't throw them away."

KEY

The efforts one invests in a given task will generally have two products: a useful portion along with waste. It is important to know and differentiate between the two. Obviously, being concerned with and consuming the waste will only prove to be futile. Similarly, clinging to practices once they have performed their intended function will be a waste of time. This applies not only to mystical training but also to the day to day life. This is similar to the advice about leaving the raft on the shore after one has crossed the river. Traditionally, this story is recounted when someone takes an action contrary to the accepted methods and rules of conduct in the community.

Spiritual nourishment is essentially a gift, though we must still work to assimilate it. But someone who thinks that spiritual grace or *baraka* is his personal possession because he has bought and paid for it with his own efforts will end by consuming much that cannot be assimilated: imperfect personalities, limited circumstances, all sorts of demands and scruples, the whole world of 'I and they'—all the waste material that obscures God's Mercy. As Omar Khayyam said, "Take the cash in hand and leave the rest."

39

MULLA NASRUDIN AND THE CARPENTER

Nasrudin was once asked if he had ever met anyone as stupid as himself.

He said, "Yes. I once had a carpenter make a door for me. When he came over to measure the frame, he forgot his ruler. So he stretched out his arms to get the width and then proceeded to start for the market to buy the materials needed. The entire way, he held his arms still trying to make sure no one bumped into him and messed up his measurements. As he got close to the market, he was so intent on holding his arms still that he forgot to watch the road and fell off into a ditch. People rushed over to help him but instead of reaching up for help, he held his arms out so as to not lose the measurement and insisted that he be pulled out by his beard. This, I think shows he is more stupid than I."

"Really? How so, Mulla?"

"He could have asked to be pulled out by his legs!"

KEY

It would have been easier for the carpenter to correct his first mistake by returning and finding a ruler of his own. However, he might have had to accept that he was wrong and that could have hurt his pride. As a result of his pride, this carpenter is constantly getting himself into deeper problems! Mulla—learned man—not willing to admit this folly searches for a face-saving solution. Perhaps 'stupidity' is relative to the topic under discussion.

Also, when we try to act as our own criterion, instead of relying on an objective criterion like the Holy Book or the guidance of a spiritual master, great mental effort and self-sacrifice may produce only negative and shameful results. The beard is the overgrowth of mere words, but the legs are something reliable that one can stand upon.

40

MULLA AND THE PUPIL

One day, one of the pupils in Nasrudin's school of theology was sitting by the courtyard pond playing with a coin when he accidentally dropped it into the water. The fountain was too deep for him to reach into, so he decided to try to pick the coin up by making it stick to the end of his walking cane.

Nasrudin saw the boy struggling at the pond and came over to investigate. "What are you doing?" he asked the pupil. "Ah teacher, I have dropped my coin into the pond. I need it back for my lunch money. I am trying to get it to stick to the end of my cane but it won't do it."

Nasrudin looked over the situation. "It is actions like this that gives us all a bad name!" Nasrudin boomed. "I am glad I was around to see this and correct your actions before you did something like this where everyone could see what fools we have here as students. Getting your coin out is a simple task. All you have to do is wet the end of your cane with saliva and then the coin will stick to it and you can pull it out."

KEY

It is not enough to have a technique to do something. One has to know when and under what conditions the technique will work. This applies to everything from using your walking stick to pick things up to when, where and how one is to pray or meditate.

And the spittle of long-winded preaching will never draw out the precious thing that has been lost in the depths of life. If water is knowledge, speech is two drops of spittle; but life is a fountain.

41

NASRUDIN ON FIRE

Once upon a time, Nasrudin was served a dish prepared with a great amount of chili peppers. He took one bite and screamed, "Someone pour water into me! I have caught fire!"

KEY

There is nothing unusual about thinking that something that really impacts only a small portion of our life is about to consume all of it. (On the other hand, it just might. Fire spreads.)

42

WEARING BLACK

Once, Mulla Nasrudin's friends saw him wearing a black robe. They wondered why.

"Ah yes," replied Nasrudin to their questions, "I am mourning the death of my son's father."

KEY

Certain Mystical Orders give their members a black robe as a symbol of spiritual awakening. Since Nasrudin is wearing such a robe, he has 'died' to the world and is thus morning his own passing.

Note that had Nasrudin said, "I am mourning myself," he would have made a nonsensical statement. Thus by stating his thoughts in this manner, he has separated his enlightened being from the being of his ego and its attachment to the material world.

(And also his attachment to having died to it).

43

BORROWING A POT

One day, Nasrudin borrowed a large cooking pot from his neighbor. Before returning it, he put a smaller pot into it and gave the two pots to the owner.

"Oh, what's this?" Asked the neighbor as he looked at the smaller pot.

"Your pot gave birth last night. So the smaller pot is yours."

The neighbor felt good about his gain and took the two pots inside. A few days later, Nasrudin asked to borrow the same large pot again. Gladly, the neighbor lent it. This time though, Mulla didn't bring it back. After a few days, the dismayed owner went to ask about his pot.

"I'm sorry to tell you this but your pot has died," Nasrudin said.

"What? How can a pot die?" asked the unbelieving neighbor.

"The same way it gave birth to another pot!" replied Nasrudin as he shut the door.

KEY

If you insist that an inanimate object can have a life of its own, you can hardly complain when it goes and does something every living thing does. This is particularly the case when you have used such an assertion for your own gain. When deciding to believe something that makes no sense, perhaps you should push the logic to the extreme and see what you come up with.

Also, it's always best to keep your life—your vitality, your knowledge, your virtue—in a single vessel; this is what is meant by being 'centered'. If your vessel 'gives birth' to another one—if you divide your life between more than one 'center'—then the 'baby pot' will decrease the capacity of the 'mother pot', and also prove to be of lesser capacity in itself. Thus, what seems to be an increase in capacity will actually prove to be a diminishment. This is what happens when someone has 'too many irons in the fire'. Such a person may believe that to scatter his or her energy indicates an increase in capacity, while the reverse is actually the case. In order to retain the largest possible capacity, one needs for all the parts of life of one's life to be gathered together in one place; this is what it means to be 'recollected'.

44

NASRUDIN'S STORK

Once, Mulla Nasrudin bought a stork. When he brought the bird home, he realized that the legs and beak were too long. So he decided to shorten them. Afterward, he wondered why the stork died.

KEY

Most people find this story plainly stupid. But then if you stop and think of the jobs, opportunities or even relationships you have lost because you tried to change someone, you might not find this such a stupid story after all.

Furthermore, if Nasrudin believed that a stork's legs and beak were too long, why didn't he buy a chicken instead? He thought he wanted a long-distance bird, but he was only fooling himself. This is a story about people who falsely believe that they possess spiritual aspiration, when all they really want is to cut the Spirit down to their own size, and end by killing it.

45

MULLA'S JOKE

It is told that once a greedy man asked Nasrudin over for dinner. The man had heard that doing something for Nasrudin would often bring good luck. Having insight, Nasrudin realized what the man was up to. He even promised to say a special prayer for the man in appreciation for the meal. The two sat down to eat and Nasrudin proceeded to stuff his face as quickly as his hands could move.

The greedy man could hardly believe his eyes. "You certainly have a big appetite. You are not even chewing each bite before you take another."

"This is true my friend but please understand, I am saying a complete prayer for you between each bite."

KEY

Often, an enlightened person will act in a way that reflects someone's own behavior back to them. Often having someone see how they look to the rest of the world is enough to wake them up (a little).

46

CATCHING GEESE

A group of geese were sitting by a pond when Mulla decided to run over and catch one. Of course, he was not fast enough and they all flew away. Disappointed, Mulla took a piece of bread from his bag and dunked it in the pond and ate it saying, "If I can't have any of the meat, at least I can enjoy the broth."

KEY

This is a sort of inverted 'sour grapes'. Often, when someone doesn't get what they want, they somehow convince themselves that what they do have is still good enough. Of course, such a positive attitude doesn't protect one from taking an absurdity as consolation.

47

EATING BEANS

Mulla Nasrudin was invited to a dinner. After the food was served, a dish of beans was brought out for the guests. Mulla pulled the dish close to himself and ate a large portion. Other guests exclaimed that if he ate too many beans, he would surely die. Nasrudin paused for a moment to reflect and then said, "If God willing I die, please make sure you treat my wife well." Then he went back to eating.

KEY

This story provides two reference points: one from Mulla's view and the second from the guests' view. The more Mulla eats, the less would be the share of other guests. One way to solve this dilemma is to stop Mulla from eating more than his own share. This, however, is contrary to the code of Chivalry—which people in the Middle East used to (and to some extent still do) abide by. Thus, the guests come up with an absurd excuse and Mulla—seeing through the absurdity— counters it by an appeal to their sense of chivalry for taking care of his family when he has departed.

People's habit of hiding their intentions behind the most absurd arguments is not limited to Mulla's friends, his society and times.

48

GOING FOR FOOD

Someone told Mulla Nasrudin, "Come to my house and I will break bread with you." Thinking of a free meal, Mulla agreed and went along.

When Mulla arrived at the host's house, the host took out bread and salt. Meanwhile, a beggar came by the door and asked for alms. The host told him to go away but the beggar insisted. The host became angry saying, "If you don't leave I will break your leg."

At that moment, Mulla called out to the beggar, "You better hurry up and leave. This man is quite sincere in what he says."

KEY

Nasrudin is not really interested in seeing the beggar fed. Of course, being able to express his concerns to the beggar and at the same time reserve all the food for himself has its advantages. Need it be pointed out how often organizations (or individuals) stand by and let something happen (even if it is wrong) because they stand to benefit from the occurrence?

There is another point that needs to be brought out. Throughout this book, we have tried to clarify the allegories used in each story. Interesting enough, here Nasrudin has come across someone who cannot communicate through the use of allegories, and anything said must be taken at face value.

49

A CONVERSATION WITH A CHRISTIAN

A Christian man was eating meat during the period of lent which was an illicit act according to his creed. Nasrudin saw what he was doing and went over to share some of the food. The Christian rebuffed him by saying, "What do you mean Mulla? Christian meat is illicit for you Muslims!"

Nasrudin instantly replied, "I am among the Muslims as you are among the Christians."

KEY

There is an old folklore saying, "Drop a dog in rose water and it's still a dog." So too, a hypocrite is what he (or she) is regardless of their confessed beliefs. And how often do we find ourselves worrying about someone else's impurity of heart so as to avoid looking at our own? On the other hand, those who understand the 'meat' of religion will not be separated by rite and creed, however important and necessary these may be on their own level.

50

BEATING THE COW

Once a cow came to Nasrudin's farm and began grazing on his crops. The Mulla snatched up a stick and chased the cow away. A few days later, Nasrudin went to the market and saw the same cow. He picked up a stick and began beating the poor beast. Its owner protested. Nasrudin said, "Be quiet! Don't you see, this animal is keeping quiet because it knows of its own crime!"

KEY

It is doubtful that the cow remembers the reason for the beating. So too, on a positive note, one should not always expect everyone to understand what is behind his actions because there is a very real difference in people's ability to see into a situation. However, one has to remember that some people do things dictated by their nature and upbringing and not because they are aware of their actions.

And if the cow's silence is a kind of confession, then for the Mulla to tell the cow's owner to be quiet is also to ask him to consider his own possible guilt in letting his cow graze on other people's crops. Loud blame (even of oneself) may really be no more than flight from the inner silence where— God willing—one may encounter true remorse.

51

MOURNING THEIR MOTHER

Nasrudin had a hen with lots of chicks. One day, the hen suddenly died. Nasrudin tied pieces of black fabric around each chick. When he was asked why, he replied, "They are mourning their mother's death."

KEY

The chicks had probably forgotten about their mother before Nasrudin tied on the black cloths. So too, there is a question of exactly what (if any) thought a chick gives death. People are very similar.

We often project our likes as well as dislikes onto others and expect that they need to follow our expectations.

Nor can our own vigilance or discernment be applied to another with much hope that he or she will understand; moral exhortations are usually no more effective than tying mourning bands on immature chickens. The admonished one may make an outward show of repentance, but that's as far as it usually goes. This is why Nasrudin teaches indirectly, but much more forcibly, by performing symbolic actions and setting up revealing situations.

52

NASRUDIN'S SICKNESS

Mulla became ill and thought he might die. He asked his friends to bury him in an old grave. When they asked him why, he replied, "On the day of judgment, the angels will come to question everyone. Maybe they will be fooled into questioning the old occupant of the grave and leave me be."

KEY

Nasrudin's desire to miss judgment day's questioning says a lot about his faith. If he really believed that everything was going to work out the way his religion said, then why would he want to be left alone? Of course, one doesn't have to look very far to see the same mind set operate today. For example, why would someone who claimed to be spiritual be overly concerned with their diet and health? Are not these things strictly physical, which is the very thing spirituality is not?

This story is also saying that one should not "rest on one's laurels" by relying on old acts of asceticism. The fact that one has died to oneself in the past doesn't mean much if one has since come back to life. On the other hand, if one's death was true—if it really was *fana'* or spiritual annihilation—then one may happily come back to life with no qualms, since one is then at the station of *baqa'*, 'subsistence in God'. Repentance and judgment are left behind with the dead body of one's ego, if one has truly 'repented of repentance'.

53

NASRUDIN'S WIFE

Once, Nasrudin had to attend a service so he gave his wife some money and asked her to go buy some meat. Then he left. On the way to the market, his wife ran into her lover and since her husband would be gone most of the day, the two of them went back to her house. No sooner had Nasrudin's wife and her lover begun enjoying each other's company than the neighbors burst into the bedroom and took them both to court. The judge ruled that the wife should be tied upside down on a donkey and paraded through the city in disgrace. Meanwhile, Nasrudin came home and not finding his wife, went looking for her. He finally found her and seeing her riding upside-down on a donkey, asked what had happened. "Oh, be quiet!" she exclaimed. "I've been to almost every market in the city and still haven't found your meat. I've only got two more to go to then I'll be home!"

KEY

Like many Nasrudin stories, this one has a very practical lesson. If you want someone to overlook something you have done, put them on the defensive. After all, didn't Nasrudin send his wife out and was not she trying to do something for him when she ended up under the donkey? Although we know that she wasn't, perhaps she is betting that Nasrudin doesn't have such complete knowledge.

This is also a story of addiction. Some people can't see the need for changing old vices, even after exposure and public shame. They still place all their hopes in trying to get their 'sin' *right* the next time.

54

BORROWING MULLA'S DONKEY

Someone came to Mulla to borrow his donkey. Nasrudin told him to wait so he would have a chance to go ask the donkey's opinion. Mulla went out to the stable and when he returned he said, "The donkey said not to lend him because the borrower would ride him while cursing his owner and beating him to move faster."

KEY

On the surface, one would conclude that Nasrudin was making a very bad excuse for not lending his donkey. On another level, however, Nasrudin's reply looks a lot like the reason why a teacher might turn down a prospective student. All too often, a student will criticize the exercises assigned to him because results are not coming fast enough or the exercises are not what was wanted (instead of what was needed).

On the other hand, we usually tend to resist placing our soul into the hands of a teacher for fear that he will put it through a difficult purgation; such a teacher might also see through our social mask and accuse us—rightly—of the sins of our 'donkey'.

55

FINDING FAULT WITH OTHER PEOPLE'S BELONGINGS

Nasrudin took his old sheet to market hoping to sell it quickly. Someone came by and said, "This sheet is full of holes. You should take it to a flea market to sell as scrap."

The Mulla replied, "You are not a buyer. Do not find faults with other people's belongings. I just took this sheet off of my comforter and up until now, not even a pinch of cotton had fallen out (of the comforter)."

KEY

Mulla's opinion of his sheet looks curiously like the opinion some people hold of ideas which, although full of holes, keep them happy and self-satisfied. Although it would seem proper to point out to them that they are clinging to idea with no substance, the question is, should we really point this out to them?

56

NASRUDIN'S WIFE AND HER LOVER

A man had become close to Nasrudin's wife. One day, he sent a good looking young man to take a message to Mulla's wife that she should make herself up and wait for him. The wife liked the messenger so much, she asked him to stay so they could have a good time together. A little later, the lover showed up. Nasrudin's wife hid the young man and tried to flirt with her lover. Meanwhile, Mulla opened the door and came in the courtyard. Immediately, the wife handed her lover a sword and said, "Be rough with me and demand I hand over your slave boy." He did. At that moment, Nasrudin came in the room and inquired what was going on. The lover shouted that his slave had escaped and this woman had hidden him. Seeing this, Nasrudin begged the man for forgiveness and let them leave.

KEY

Here is a case where Nasrudin's wife gets what she wants and outsmarts both her lover and her husband. In Mysticism, there are many things that can attract one's attention and efforts. One can fall for the exercises and activities of a group (the messenger) or one can become so enamored with a teacher (the lover) that they forget the real objective of the project (the mystical marriage). If this happens, the spiritual task will be mis-defined. False submission to false demands may use up all our provisions for the journey.

57

NASRUDIN'S PARTY

Once upon a time, there was a party in which everyone was to bring their lover. It so happened that Nasrudin's wife was a lover of one of the men at the party so she was invited to attend. Unknown to her, her husband was also invited to the party.

Upon entering the room, she saw him and began wailing, "You wretched man! You leave me hungry with no support at home while you spend your days in parties like this!" She then gave someone some money and asked them to bring a judge so she could divorce Nasrudin on the spot. As everyone waited for the judge, some of the people present tried to intervene and get the couple back together. Finally, Nasrudin offered to make an oath to never attend such parties in the future and his wife agreed to forget the entire matter.

The two left the party and headed home. About half way there, the wife pulled up short, swearing an oath that since Nasrudin had misbehaved, she would not go home that day. Already in enough trouble, Nasrudin went on alone. His wife, on the other hand, went back to the party and had a wonderful time.

KEY

Not unlike the previous story, there are several levels to this story. On the surface, it does show one way to get yourself out of trouble. On another, it illustrates the habit people have of wasting time on activities that have no lasting value. Nasrudin may have thought he would enjoy the party but probably never stopped to think what it could cost him if he got caught. In the same vein, we may enjoy the quick emotional high of meeting strange new people or wearing strange new cloths or changing out diet but how many actually stop and ask if such activities have any lasting value or may even do more harm than good.

This story also shows how our vices can sometimes be 'self-righteous' in their demands, claiming their 'rights' and making us ashamed not to satisfy them—and how it is these vices, not us, that derive pleasure from their satisfaction. The addict 'feeds his addiction,' not himself.

58

NASRUDIN'S WIFE AND SATAN

Late one night, Mulla Nasrudin's wife decided to go for a walk. Someone asked her, "Aren't you afraid to be out alone at this time of night?"

To this she answered, "Well, no. If a man gets hold of me, that's exactly why I left home in the first place. If Satan comes my way, well, we are already old friends."

KEY

Fear of something can be useful for restraining some people. However, if a person has lost their fear, they can be impossible to control. People who have no fear of destruction may often exhibit a great fear of the very thing that could save them.

59

MULLA NASRUDIN AND THE PROPHET'S TRADITIONS

When he had reached old age, Nasrudin was asked if he remembered any of the sayings of the Prophet as being especially meaningful to him. The Mulla replied that he knew a

Tradition retold by Akrama, which no one else had heard. The people became excited at the prospect of hearing a never-before-heard tradition and pressed Nasrudin to tell it.

"I have heard," started Nasrudin, "it being related that Akrama had heard it from Ibn Abbas who heard it from the Prophet Muhammad who said, 'There are two personality traits which are not seen in the human being unless he is a true believer.'"

Excitedly, everyone pressed the Mulla to tell about them. "Well, you see, Akrama had forgotten one, I have forgotten the other."

KEY

Have you ever felt the urge to say something to attract attention to yourself? Here Nasrudin does exactly that. Attention is an often-overlooked part of whatever is going on. Often people cannot go through life unless they receive a certain amount of attention from others (and generally such people become actors, teachers or engage in some other profession that requires people to pay attention to them). So the next time someone does something unexpected, stop and ask yourself if their real intention was simply to attract a little attention to themselves.

There is another consideration. A number of times, information must be transmitted to those who have the capacity to understand. Otherwise, the teacher would be burdened with a barrage of quizzical comments and inquiries. Claiming ignorance or forgetfulness is a good defense in these situations.

There is a certain sort of professor who is adept at making a parade of knowledge without actually imparting any. Yet there may be a good reason for suggesting a truth without making it entirely explicit. If the people were told the character traits of a true believer, they would likely use this knowledge to judge or idolize each other—and how many of us are objective enough to ask ourselves whether or not we possess such traits, and then give a true answer?

60

MULLA'S DINNER

Once Nasrudin brought home two pounds of meat and asked his wife what type of dish could be prepared with the meat.

His wife said, "any type."

"Okay then, make the 'any type' dish."

KEY

When pursuing personal development programs, often people imitate Nasrudin here. Rather than ask specific questions like "what kind of business is the teacher in?" they unthinkingly take whatever they are given and blindly follow it.

People tend to have a very vague idea of the goal of the mystical path, since they haven't gotten there yet. And with little idea of the goal, how can they understand the method? This can lead to a lifetime of vague longings and gestures that are indulged in only because they seem to be 'spiritual' in one way or another. The lower self loves this kind of thing, which allows it to consider itself spiritual without taking even one step toward its own 'transformation'.

61

MULLA'S ANSWER

Someone once asked Mulla Nasrudin, "Each month, the moon waxes and wanes and then a new moon comes out. What happens to the old moon?"

"Oh stupid! The old moon is crushed into pieces and made into stars!" replied Mulla.

KEY

What happens when the founder of a great movement dies? The movement splinters into countless little groups, each reflecting some little aspect of what was taught. Of course, there is a case to be made that the light reflected by such a fragment is still of much use.

The moon goes through phases, but the stars are fixed. After a great movement—or any created being for that matter—completes its cycle of birth and death, it returns to its eternal 'constellation'.

62

EATING LIVER

Once upon a time, Mulla went to the market and bought some lamb liver. On his way home, a raven swooped down and stole the package from him. Mulla watched as the raven settled on a near-by roof and began eating the liver. As Nasrudin watched the bird, a man walked by carrying a package of liver and in an instant, Nasrudin snatched his package and ran to the top of the roof where the raven was. The victim followed him and when he caught up to Nasrudin, he demanded to know what Mulla was doing.

"I wanted to see if I could do what the raven did," replied Nasrudin.

KEY

Blind imitation is more popular than most people realize. How many people have tried to learn such practices as yoga or meditation from a book or a video tape? Do they really understand if what they are doing is what they need to do? It should be noted that the idea that all one needs is a mantra and a schedule of practice (which is identical to everyone else's) has had some popularity in the past. Of course, if that was all it took to realize the truth, one suspects that someone would have stumbled across the proper set formula thousands of years ago and mankind would be rid of the problems that still confront it.

63

MULLA'S EXCUSE (1)

A neighbor wanted to borrow Nasrudin's rope. Mulla said that he could not lend it because his wife was drying sesame seeds on it.

"What do you mean?" exclaimed the neighbor, "No one dries seeds on a rope!"

"That's not true. When you don't want to lend your rope, you dry seeds on it, or flour, or…"

KEY

Social codes of conduct dictate that members of society must help when someone is in need. This extends to lending of tools and other items to neighbors and friends. However, it is common knowledge that most people do not take care of a borrowed object the same way as the owner. Thus, one feels that once an object is lent, the lender may not see it again!

How would one balance the social obligation to help with the fear of losing one's property? Mulla's answer is to come up with the most absurd excuses!

And how often does our sense of something's value depend upon the feeling that we own it? If we want someone to value us, we often try to make them jealous in an attempt to awaken this sense of ownership in them. But if something is not valued for its intrinsic qualities, it cannot be put to any real use.

64

MULLAS'S EXCUSE (2)

One day, a neighbor came over to ask if he could borrow Mulla's shovel.

"I'm sorry," said Mulla, "I cannot lend it to you. You see, my shovel has swallowed."

"What are you talking about?" asked the neighbor. "Shovels can't swallow."

"If don't want to lend them, they can."

KEY

Sometimes it does little good to try to say no to someone gently. Often, whoever we are talking to simply lacks the sensitivity to catch the real meaning of what we are trying to say to them without having to come right out with it. Being gentle and indirect does offer the benefit of not having to confront someone with something they don't want to hear. It also makes it possible for them to misunderstand or intentionally overlook what you are saying.

But there may be another meaning here: possessions, whether material or immaterial, do tend to swallow us. To be possessive of something is also to be possessed by it.

65

MULLA NASRUDIN'S DEATH

One day, Nasrudin climbed a tree and began sawing the branch he was sitting on. A man passed by, saw what he was doing and pointed out that Mulla would fall if he continued. Disregarding the advice, Mulla kept sawing and sure enough a few minutes later, he came crashing to the ground. Shocked by the man's prediction coming true, Nasrudin ran after him. When he caught up, he said, "If you knew my fate, then you surely know when I will die!"

Recognizing Mulla's stupidity, the man replied, "Oh yes! You shall die when your donkey passes gas three times in a row."

It just so happened that a few days later, Nasrudin put a heavy load on his donkey and headed for the hills. At the base of the hills, the poor donkey began struggling with the load and exerting itself to its fullest, it passed gas. Alarmed, Nasrudin thought he felt his life force move up to his knees. He sat down. As the donkey struggled on, it let more gas loose.

"Oh no!" exclaimed Nasrudin, "my soul is at chest level!"

The donkey took one more step and passed gas a third time. Nasrudin cried, "Oh no, I am dead!" He laid on the ground motionless as his donkey wandered away.

A short while later, some friends came by and saw him motionless on the ground. When they asked what was going on, Nasrudin recounted the entire story.

For fun, Mulla's buddies found an old casket, put Nasrudin in it and began carrying him back to town. On the way, they came across a body of water which they could not cross. Mulla raised his head from the casket and said, "The passage is from such and such direction. When I was alive I used to use it a lot. You can use it if you like."

KEY

Mulla refuses to recognize his own folly. When the outcome of his actions is predicted by other members of his community, he takes their words as the words of sages and prophets and insists on following them—still refusing to acknowledge the consequences of his own actions. We could learn a lot by developing a greater flexibility of mind.

66

DRIVING A NAIL IN THE WALL

Once, Mulla was driving a nail into the wall of his barn. He used too much strength and the nail went completely through the wall and out the other side. Now, right next to Nasrudin's barn was his neighbor's barn and the nail went through that barn's wall as well. Nasrudin looked through the hole and saw dozens of horses and donkeys in the other barn. Happily he ran to his wife shouting, "Come look! I have found a stable full of horses and donkeys. I believe someone must have hidden them there long ago!"

KEY

It would probably be uncharitable to suggest that Mulla's actions resemble some people's when they have happened to come upon some idea that is new to them but commonplace to everyone else. Not only do they overlook the basic everyday explanation of what they have learned, but often they will let over-worked emotions keep them from taking a real world look at their new situation.

Furthermore, to glimpse a truth does not necessarily mean that this truth is effectively available to us; in order to use a truth it must belong to us, and it can only belong to us if Truth Itself has permitted us to know it, and if we have paid the price that Truth demands. (As one poet said, "Like everything else I have / Somebody showed it to me / And I found it by myself.")[1] Other people's religions, other people's paths in life, as well as 'ancient truths' from religions dead and gone, will not carry us a single step. At best they are an interesting entertainment; at worse, a fatal distraction.

67

NOT SPEAKING THE LANGUAGE

Once upon a time, Mulla Nasrudin traveled to a far off village. Even though he did not speak the villagers' language, one of the eminent people invited him to dinner. Nasrudin

1. Lew Welch, from the poem 'Wobbly Rock', contained in his collected poems, *Ring of Bone*.

put on his best suit and took along his servant. At the dinner, there was so much delicious food that Nasrudin lost control of himself and ate much more than his share. The combination of strange foods and a too full stomach caused Mulla pain and he could not control himself and passed gas with a loud noise.

As they were returning to their own village, Mulla's servant told him that his actions were rude and uncalled for.

Nasrudin reassured him, "Don't worry. Since they were too dumb to understand our language, they would also not understand my action!"

KEY

Nasrudin's behavior looks not unlike that of many self-proclaimed students of higher learning. Although they go to a teacher wanting to acquire learning, they want what is taught to them according to their expectations, when they want it, in the amount they want it, and they really expect that the teacher will not see right though their attitude.

68

MULLA'S GUESS

One day a man hid an egg in his hand and told Mulla, "If you tell me what I am hiding, I will make an omelet out of it and give it to you."

Nasrudin asked for some hints.

The man replied that it was white on the outside and yellow in the center.

Mulla replied, "I know. It must be a turnip which has been cored out and filled with carrots!"

KEY

Sometimes we are so focused on a 'bee line' approach to accomplishing a task that we do not see alternatives when an obstacle prevents us from achieving our goal in a direct manner. In a way, one needs to see both the trees and the woods.

Here, Mulla is so focused on getting the prize that he completely ignores the clue (omelet) and tries to come up with the most ridiculous solutions. What is most obvious is often the hardest thing for us to see—especially if we are addicted to mysteries and secrets.

69

MULLA NASRUDIN'S TRADING

One day, Mulla was passing through a market when someone asked him if it was the third or fourth day of the month. Nasrudin replied that he did not know because he had not traded days in a long time.

KEY

If we put someone in the position of knowledge and author-ity, they may develop the expectation that they should have all the answers all the times. Otherwise, they have lost face.

Here with Mulla in the market place, people are trading goods. To appear knowledgeable, he thinks he has to adopt the language of a merchant!

But maybe the Mulla's answer is not as foolish as it sounds. On one level, the answer to the merchant's question is always 'today'. Those who trade days are trying to get a 'bet-ter deal' out of life by living in the past or the future, forget-ting that all successful business transactions take place only 'today'.

70

GREETINGS

One day, Mulla Nasrudin came across a stranger and said hello.

The stranger was surprised and asked, "Who are you and how do you know me?"

Mulla replied, "I have never seen you before but your robe and turban look like mine so I thought you might be me!"

KEY

Mistaking appearance for substance is common enough. Just because some may happen to follow the same rituals as you do does not mean that they in fact share your beliefs.

And there is a character type, called a 'narcissist', who can only relate to someone if he or she identifies with that person. But can we really call this state of affairs a 'relationship'?

71

MULLA NASRUDIN AND THE DAY OF RESURRECTION

Once upon a time, Mulla was on a walk when he passed an old graveyard. The graveyard was outside the city and no one was about. Looking around, Mulla spotted an empty grave and became curious about how it would feel to be dead. So he climbed down into the grave and stretched out.

It just so happened that a caravan came by and Mulla sat up out of the grave to see what was going on. The sight of a man coming out of a grave frightened some of the people and their screams scarred the horses and camels. All the animals ran away, their loads fell off and were scattered on the ground. Angered, some of the men from the caravan came over and beat the living daylights out of Nasrudin. Finally, Nasrudin managed to escape and run home. Seeing his tattered appearance, his wife asked what had happened. Mulla replied that he had come back from the Day of Judgment.

"And how are people treated on that day?" She asked.

Mulla answered, "If you leave the animals alone, they leave you alone."

KEY

Magic thinking is no more rare today than in Nasrudin's time. Everyone knows someone who has a lucky charm. Failing to see the obvious connection between an action and its result is a common behavior. If you don't pay your power bills and the local provider cuts your lights off, this does not mean that the devil or his legions are acting against you.

On another level, this story teaches that to treat the transformation of the ego as if it were a mere pastime, something we are free to take or leave alone, is to wreak havoc in both the psyche and the social world. (This caution applies particularly to various methods of seeking transcendence of the ego as a personal experience, which is obviously a contradiction in terms.)

On a further level, the story shows how threatening a true spiritual path is to the habitual ways of the world, as if a person were to be warned: "If you continue with this unselfish behavior, you'll ruin things for all of us!" The lower self of society (the animals in the caravan) can smell the death of the lower self in an individual—and, as the contemporary saying goes, "no good deed goes unpunished." This is why it is sometimes necessary to hide one's spiritual states not just from society, but from one's own lower self; this is what Jesus meant by "not letting your right hand know what your left hand is doing."

72

SELLING A LADDER

One day, Mulla took a ladder to an orchard, climbed over the wall, propped it against the nearest tree and climbing it again, began harvesting some fruit.

The owner came by and asked Nasrudin what he was doing. Mulla angrily replied, "Don't you see? I'm selling ladders!"

Unbelieving, the owner asked, "Is this a place for trading ladders?"

"Oh fool," thundered Nasrudin, "don't you know one may sell ladders anywhere?"

KEY

True, one can do all sorts of things just about anywhere. But some places are better designed for some activities than others. If someone seems to be doing something that really doesn't belong in the setting they are doing it in, then perhaps their motives should be questioned. People hide their intentions and once their defensive lines are threatened, they tend to lash back even though they may be in the wrong.

On another level, ladders may represent forms of the spiritual path; the fruit is the goal of the path. Ladders are indeed being sold everywhere these days. If these ladders are being sold only to help us to steal spiritual fruit, if we are using them in an attempt to reach the goal by our own unguided efforts, or taking them as methods for stealing truths and practices from traditions that do not belong to us, then we are putting ourselves in danger of being arrested as thieves—and rightly so.

Still, there is a sense in which ladders can legitimately be sold anywhere, in that every experience in life can be turned to spiritual profit—if we possess the key.

73

MULLA NASRUDIN'S MOVE

One night, Mulla Nasrudin was sleeping when a thief came in, collected his few belongings and left. Mulla got up, grabbed his bed and followed the thief to his house.

When they both entered, the thief angrily asked, "What are you doing here?"

"Oh nothing," calmly replied Mulla, "I have just moved my residence. Here is some money for your efforts."

KEY

Every now and then it is a good idea to read a Nasrudin story from the perspective of the other people involved. Can you imagine how the thief must feel here? In Islamic countries, the criminal justice system has a singular way of punishing wrongdoing. So unless the thief wants to risk punishment, he is stuck with Nasrudin (who incidentally here shows a very clever way of turning a situation to his advantage).

Vices usually flourish in areas of our psyche where we are not paying full attention. To place one's spiritual attention on one of these gray areas is to neutralize it, because if the vice rebels when in the presence of spiritual authority, it knows it will be punished; therefore it becomes quiet. Furthermore, what is a vice when we are unconscious of it, after we have become aware of it may turn out to be a hidden aspect of our soul that actually has a legitimate claim on us— though not, of course, a claim to everything we own.

74

THE OTHER SIDE OF THE TREE

Once upon a time, three children were passing through an alley when they saw Nasrudin coming in their direction. They decided to trick Mulla into giving up his shoes. They went over to a big tree and called out to Mulla, "Oh no! No one has ever climbed a tree this big!" Having heard this, Mulla came over and said he could do it.

To this the youngsters said, "Words are one thing but actions are another. Show us if you can."

Nasrudin agreed and took off his shoes so he could climb better. But instead of leaving them on the ground at the base of the tree, he slipped them into his pocket and carried them with him.

From below, the children called out, "Why are you taking your shoes, Mulla?"

"Because," he called down, "There might be a road to the other side from here."

KEY

In any encounter, one has to maintain a certain sense of balance and presence of mind. Often, we are praised for having abilities or talents which subsequently must be demonstrated and/or proven. We need to maintain the presence of mind not to be lulled into a situation where someone might take advantage of us.

On the other hand, there really might be a road up there. Climbing a tree can symbolize a spiritual state—one initiated by children, in this case, who could indicate something unplanned and spontaneous, since spiritual states are considered to be gifts, not acquisitions. But just because a high state has come over us, we should not forget the need for spiritual labor. Once we have reached a new level, we must not rest, but be prepared to continue walking the path by our own efforts. This is how a temporary state (*hal*) can become a permanent station (*maqam*).

75

MULLA'S CLOTHING

One day, Mulla attended a gathering. He was wearing his normal day-to-day clothes. Once he entered the gathering, no one noticed him. A few minutes later, Mulla left without saying a word and went home. There, he changed into an expensive outfit and went back to the gathering. Upon arriving, the host announced Mulla's arrival and gave him the best seat in the room. As soon as everyone was seated, expensive dishes were brought out and served. Mulla reached over and put his sleeve in first one dish and then another.

"What are you doing?" asked the host.

"Since you only pay respect to those in fancy clothes," replied Mulla, "It goes without saying that the food is really prepared for the clothes."

KEY

A very good illustration of how one could fool others into accepting one as someone s/he is not. If you want to be seen in a certain way, adopt the clothing and manners of that someone. Few people will bother to really look and see if there is anything behind your appearance. This strategy has made more than a few fake 'wise men' wealthy.

By this tale, Mulla may not be proposing dishonesty; rather, this joke is often relayed when a group of fake and superficial people is encountered.

[Once in the 1960s a darvish was traveling through the USA with a couple of his hippy friends. At dusk they parked their truck on a hill above the town of Elko, Nevada, and prepared to go to sleep. Then they saw a car full of young cowboys driving up, obviously getting ready to hassle or maybe even beat up the hippies. All the cowboys had on black cowboy hats. As they got out of the car and approached in a menacing manner, the darvish suddenly put on a black cowboy hat that happened to be in the back of the truck. The cowboys all stopped short as if paralyzed, looked at each other in bewilderment, then got back in their car and drove away.]

76

MULLA'S RIDDLE

Once, Mulla gave the following riddle to his students:

"Suppose that two oxen want to pass through a narrow alley and it so happens that their horns get tangled. Which of the two oxen can claim that they have their horns stuck underneath the other?"

Some of the students said, "the first ox" and Mulla disagreed. Then they said "the second ox," and Mulla shook his head again. Finally, they said, "Then both." Mulla still disagreed. Lost, the students asked what the solution was.

"Neither of the two," said Mulla, "oxen do not talk."

KEY

It is probably a very lucky thing that oxen cannot talk; if they could, a large number of them might get their horns so entangled while arguing about who had the higher horns that they could never free themselves, and die in this wretched state.

When faced by difficult situations, Mulla teaches us not to rush to a solution and keep the 'whole picture' in mind before making any suggestions.

77

MULLA NASRUDIN'S PRESENT

Once upon a time, someone gave Nasrudin some plums. Now, since this took place during that time of the year when plums are rare, Mulla decided to take some of the fruit and give them to the mayor of his city. Placing the plums in a dish, Nasrudin set out for the mayor's court. On the way, he noticed that the plums kept shifting in the dish whereupon he told them to be still or he would be forced to eat them himself.

A little while later, Mulla noticed that the plums had not heeded his warning, and so he began eating them one by one. By the time he had arrived at the court, there was only one plum left. This one, he presented to the mayor. Since he was fond of plums, the mayor rewarded Nasrudin with a bag of silver coins.

A few days later, Nasrudin began thinking about how he could make some money. He went to the market, bought some cucumbers, and placing them in the same tray, headed back to the court. On the way, he came across a friend who suggested that cucumbers would not make a good present and that Nasrudin should rather take tomatoes.

Once in the mayor's presence, Mulla extended his hand to show his gift of tomatoes. But this time, the ruler was in a very bad mood and the sight of tomatoes angered him. He ordered his guards to take Nasrudin and throw the tomatoes at him.

Every time a tomato hit Nasrudin he cried out a thanks to the Lord. Puzzled, the mayor asked why he would do such a thing. Mulla replied, "I was going to bring nice big cucumbers but a friend stopped me and suggested tomatoes. Just think what damage hard cucumbers would have caused me. I am thanking God for that reason." The mayor laughed, gave Mulla some money and asked him to spare the court from future gifts.

KEY

There are a few points that can be considered here. First, why is it that Nasrudin assumed that just because something worked once, it would work a second time? Second, did he stop to think that the mayor's mood may have been more important that the gift? Lastly, in spite of everything, Nasrudin won out in the end. Was it blind luck or something else?

Greed got the best of Mulla, but his saving grace was that at the crucial moment—when he had the encounter with his friend—he had the flexibility of mind not to insist on his own way as being the only right way.

Also, the first gift the mayor accepted was that of a single plum. When we are carrying many 'plums'—many ideas, plans or concerns—they often interfere with each other. In normal social interactions, to give someone many gifts will seem like flattery or manipulation; a single gift is often more heartfelt. And the best gift we can give is singleness of attention.

Simplicity has such power that it invokes complexity, and that's what brings trouble. To endure the blows of complexity with gratitude while remembering God is the only way back to simplicity again. And to walk this circle back to the point where we began is to realize that only God is the Giver.

78

MULLA AND THE BOWL

Once, Mulla went to the pantry to get something to eat. When he opened the door, a bowl of onions fell on his head. Angered, he picked up the bowl and threw it against the ground as hard as he could. The bowl bounced off the ground and hit Mulla in the forehead, cutting him. Frustrated, he went into the kitchen and got a large knife. He came back demanding, "Where is the bowl? Know that I am ready to fight back!"

KEY

If people stopped doing things that were only going to harm them, then the world would be a different place. If people started to think before they acted on anger, it would be a very different place.

Someone who is unaware of his own actions will see the

events of his life either as the plotting of evil adversaries or the decree of hopeless fate. To fight other people needlessly is to make many needless enemies, while to struggle against your fate using the same actions that formed it in the first place is truly to "shoot yourself in the foot." As the Greek philosopher Heraclitus said, "character is fate."

79

THE CONSOLATION OF SHEEP

A friend once asked Mulla his birth sign. Nasrudin replied that it was the sign of the sheep. Nasrudin's friend said he had never heard of that sign. Mulla replied, "Well, when I was born, my birth sign was the lamb but I imagine by now, it has grown up to be a sheep."

KEY

Perhaps there are some things in human nature that never change despite age, education and experience. Lambs will always grow up to be sheep. But this story is probably also saying that we can't really be defined by our potential, only by what we make out of it. If we have wasted our lives, we can't take much consolation from remembering that in high school we were voted "most likely to succeed."

80

RIGHT HAND SIDE

Once Mulla had a house guest. One dark night, his guest needed to go to the outhouse to answer the call of nature. He asked Mulla if he could borrow the lamp sitting next to his right hand.

"Are you crazy?" replied Mulla, "in such a dark night, how can I tell the difference between my right and left hands?"

KEY

Although this story seems to make fun of Nasrudin's inability to know his right from his left in the dark, in fact, this tale is related to the lost ring story (number 90). Far less outside searching and far more inside searching is needed.

If we are in the dark (or are kept in the dark), can we really tell the difference between what is right and what is not?

This story is also a satire of the kind of person who has to submit everything to external criteria. When faced with an opportunity to perform an act of kindness, do we tell the potential recipient to wait until we have consulted the holy books and the words of the saints, and obtained a religious scholar's decree on the matter? The Heart knows right and wrong by its own light, not by anything external. But this does not mean that we are necessarily able to hear what the true spiritual Heart is telling us. And in the dark night of God's Essence, in the mystery of His will, Wrath and Mercy are not differentiated. What appears as a stroke of God's Wrath may have a hidden mercy in it, just as what seems to be an act of God's Mercy may in fact lead us astray.

81

THE DEAD MAN'S GRUDGE

Mulla had a disagreement with a man in his neighborhood. Sometime later, the man died and Nasrudin was asked to appear at his burial to say the last prayers. He refused, saying "that man held a grudge against me when he was alive and now he would obviously not listen to me."

KEY

Do people say prayers because they want to be heard by God or because they want to be heard by the people around them? Does worship require a public act or a private decision? How many of us act like Nasrudin and want to be religious only when someone else (i.e. another human being) is listening?

82

THE RESPONSIBILITY OF THE JUDGE

Two neighbors were arguing over which of them had the responsibility of picking up the corpse of a dog lying in the street. Eventually, they decided to take their case before a judge and let him decide the issue.

It so happened that Mulla Nasrudin was present and the judge asked his opinion. "Well, the street," said Mulla, "is a public property and doesn't belong to either of these two men. It is really the responsibility of the judge to take the corpse away."

KEY

This is a very good example of "watch out what and who you ask" because you never know what they are going to say.

We could add a bit of symbolism to this story: the street is the spiritual path, the neighbors are travelers on the path, God is the judge and the dog is the lower self. By looking at story from this point of view, we could say that when the lower self is dead, then it is time for the conscience to be at peace, time for inner divisions and conflicts to end. Nasrudin is right: It *is* the responsibility of the Judge to remove the dog's corpse—since it was He who killed it.

83

THE BROTH OF THE BROTH

A villager came to visit Mulla and brought him rabbit meat. Mulla had his wife cook the rabbit in broth and he treated his visitor royally. The villager returned home very happy.

A short while later, a man showed up at Mulla's door claiming to be the villager's brother. Mulla treated him warmly and a few days later the same man showed up again and was once again treated well.

It was not long until a group of people showed up claiming to be the villager's relatives or friends. Nasrudin asked them to dinner. He served them some meat and broth saying it was the meat and broth brought by the first villager. Of course, since he had already fed a few people, Nasrudin had added some water to the broth to make it go around.

A week later, another group showed up also claiming to be neighbors of the relative of the first villager. Mulla also asked them to dinner and when everyone was seated, he gave each one of them a bowl of hot water. Everyone demanded to know what was going on. Mulla explained that just as they were friends of the friends of the man with the rabbit, the water was the broth of the broth of the rabbit.

KEY

This story illustrates what happens when people try to teach from someone else's experience instead of their own. In the beginning, someone who has known a teacher may in fact have a reflection of the teacher's experience to pass along. However, since it is only a reflection and not based on personal experience, it is incomplete. In time and with each passing generation, the reflection grows dimmer and the teaching becomes dogmatic as the first experience is lost. In time, there is little or nothing left of the original teaching which offered real answers to real needs.

84

DAYS OF THIS CITY

Once upon a time, Mulla Nasrudin was visiting a foreign city. Someone came up to him and asked him what day it was, "I have just come to this city," said Mulla, "and I am not familiar with the days around here. You had better ask a local."

KEY

Have you ever hesitated to express something you knew to be true just because you were unsure of who your listeners were? There is a subtle difference between doubting what you know and doubting yourself in general.

And it is certainly true that the quality of time changes from place to place, or from group to group. When the physical or spiritual climate is different, the rhythm of life and development is also different. Actual *qualitative* time, rather than abstract *quantitative* time, is the time of the Spirit.

85

MULLA'S SON

One day, Mulla was up in the pulpit to deliver a sermon. But, regardless of how hard he thought, he could not think of anything to say. Finally, he began, "O people, you are well aware of my abilities to talk and deliver sermons but today nothing, absolutely nothing comes to me."

His son who was in the audience stood up and said, "Father, didn't you even think about leaving the pulpit?" Everyone marveled at his son and Mulla praised God for bestowing such a son on him.

KEY

No matter how good you are at something, being human insures you will (sooner or later) have an off day and not perform to your usual standards. Of course everyone knows this (but few people really take it into account).

The other side of presence with God is absence from the world. The existence of the Guide is based on his nothingness; the richness of his teaching is based on his poverty. But the thought of absence and annihilation can never arise while one is present and existent. Such a thought must arrive from somewhere else.

86

SAVING THE MOON

One night, when the moon was full, Nasrudin happened to look onto his well. There he saw the reflection of the moon. Thinking that the moon was trapped down in the well, he decided to rescue it by pulling it out. He tied a hook onto a rope and threw it into the well. The hook struck a rock and regardless of how hard Mulla pulled, the rope didn't budge. With one last titanic jerk, the rope snapped and Nasrudin fell onto his back. Looking up, he saw the moon and exclaimed, "I suffered and worked hard to save you and you don't even say 'thank you'."

KEY

There is a difference between intelligent effort and heroic effort. Often, one will spend so much effort on heroic methods that once one simply stops; the release of energy gives the impression of great development when, in fact, one has just stopped needlessly expending energy. It makes sense to examine our efforts every once in a while to ensure that we are not expending energy on useless tasks.

In this case the task is to be like the water in the well (the well is the Heart) before Nasrudin started fishing for the moon in it: still, calm, and reflective. The consciousness of God cannot be grasped; it can only be received.

87

NASRUDIN AND HIS WIFE'S DEATH

One day, Nasrudin was told his wife had died. He replied, "She was a smart and kind woman. I was about to divorce her but she did not want me to go through the hassle."

KEY

One way to look at this tale is to consider that meaning needs to be found in every difficult situation. Few things seem as pointless as the unexpected loss of a loved one. Perhaps Nasrudin is here grasping for a way to find such meaning.

Another way to consider this tale is to see Mulla as a self-centered individual who sees any situation in relationship to his own convenience.

It is clear from these stories that Nasrudin's wife usually represents the lower self, which always argues that to 'divorce' it will be much too difficult for us. In one sense this is only a lame excuse. But in another sense, the lower self may often simply 'die' on its own—by the Grace of God. The struggle against the lower self is sometimes actually carried on *by* the lower self, in a list-ditch attempt to retain its power over us; and this truly is too much of a 'hassle'. So Nasrudin's wife really was a very smart person in this story; instead of putting them both through the stress of a divorce, she simply dies. In this guise she represents not the lower self, but rather the self in submission to God, the '*nafs* at peace'. Submission to God, though it is our duty to practice it, is not something we must manufacture entirely on our own. If it were not somehow there already, in potential at least, we could never reach it.

88

FALLING DOWN

One day, Mulla was riding his donkey very fast through an alley when the donkey slipped and fell down. The children who saw this began laughing and singing, "Mulla fell down, Mulla fell down." As though nothing had happened, Mulla stood up, knocked on the nearest door and said, "I wanted to talk to this landlord anyway."

KEY

There is a real art in turning the unexpected to your advantage. Of course, Nasrudin probably doesn't know the person he is about to talk to but the children don't know that. As a result, Mulla can save face.

But this story also has a deeper meaning. Sometimes our lower self—by God's secret command—will simply fail, run out of steam. Whether on the physical or the spiritual level, this is the end of its dominion. And when it does fall down, the last thing we should do is try to get it back on its feet. The way to turn this unexpected fall to our advantage is to boldly turn toward God, the Landlord, and ask admittance to His house, seeing that He is *Lord of the worlds, Owner of the Day of Judgment.* [Qur'an 1:1:3]

89

TAKE REFUGE IN GOD

One of the rulers asked Mulla Nasrudin, "At the time of the Abbasid Caliphs, it was customary for rulers to be given titles which ended with the suffix -*God*. For example there were titles like 'who was successful by God', or 'trusted in God', or 'took help from God'. What title should people say when they see me?"

"The best thing to say," expounded Mulla, is "'I take refuge in God'."

KEY

Politicians are like this. They occasionally need to be reminded that their action do in fact impact real people in real situations. Nasrudin seems to be saying that it is best that people avoid contact with officials... a wisdom that still offers much today.

It is the true mark of the tyrant that other people are not real to him; he is 'the only game in town'. In this case the tyrant is the lower self. When the self is challenged by the presence of God, its last trick may be for it to claim to *be* God. To say "I take refuge in God" is to deny the lower self this final refuge.

90

MULLAS'S RING

Mulla lost his ring in his room. He looked for a short time but did not find it. So, he left the room and looked around the courtyard. His wife exclaimed that he had lost the ring in his room and not in the yard. Mulla agreed:

"But the room was too dark. Out here, I can see better."

KEY

On the face of it, this story seems to be saying that we often pretend to be searching for something when we are actually trying to avoid it, that our own convenience in seeking is sometimes more important to us than the object of our quest. Furthermore, mystics from all over the world have pointed out the need for people to look inside themselves to find truth—a place that is very dark for most of us until our eyes have adjusted to the shadows. Still, this has done nothing to slow down people's rush to find truth in philosophy, relationship or cult, all of which are very much outside them but at least easier to see in the light of day. Unfortunately, this does not mean that most people can see them for what they are. The light of explicit, particular knowledge can blind; the darkness of Unitive Knowledge can be a great source of light. It can teach us that to search for what we already possess is only to lose it. Although we cannot 'find' God, God has already 'found' us.

91

PULLING TEETH

Some one complained of an eye ache and he wanted a cure. Mulla replied that he had a toothache and he pulled the tooth.

KEY

People rush to offer a solution to a problem when they have not developed an appreciation for the expanse of all the issues involved. The cure must match the illness!

On the other hand, maybe this patient had a toothache because he was grinding his teeth in anger, or working them too hard trying to 'eat' his experience of the world around him. Greed and anger can blind; in order to *see* things as they are, the first requirement is to let them *be* as they are.

92

OLD MAN'S INFANT

Nasrudin was asked, "Is it possible for a wife of a hundred-year-old man to get pregnant and give birth to a boy?"

"Yes," Mulla replied, "if he has a twenty-year-old neighbor."

KEY

If something looks impossible, it probably is. Still, if the seemingly impossible happens, there still may be a very good explanation.

Habit makes us old, but God has the power to break habits. The young neighbor is like the apparition of God in the form of an Eternal Youth that the Sufi master Ibn al-'Arabi saw at the Ka'ba. In the words of Rabi'a, "first the Neighbor, then the house."

93

WHAT HAS BEEN WASTED

Someone told Mulla, "I heard your wife's reasoning abilities have been wasted." Nasrudin remained quiet, apparently in deep thought. The man asked what he was thinking so hard about.

"My wife never had any reasoning abilities," replied Mulla, "so I am wondering what part of her might *actually* have been wasted."

KEY

This reminds me of the following question, "Do you still beat your wife?" How do you answer this question without trapping yourself? If a person's reasoning abilities have been wasted, how can someone know if this person ever really had such abilities? Mulla is quite clever in that he changes the question from something intangible (her reasoning ability) into a tangible item (a part of her).

When the lower self gets hold of the rational mind, it seems as if it can reason, when all it can really do is rationalize and hatch plots. Reason is still what it is, no matter how it may have been perverted, since it is a factor of objective Truth. In essence it cannot be wasted; Truth is always what it is, and nothing else. But something else has indeed been wasted: *precious time.* And this story is also saying that if (as it were) we dig up a plant every day to see how much it has grown, we will never be successful farmers; one owes discretion to oneself as well as to others. For wisdom to mature in us, our vessel must be kept 'hermetically sealed'.

94

LACK OF COMPANY

Mulla Nasrudin went to a judge to divorce his wife. The judge asked what Mulla's wife's name was. Nasrudin replied that he did not know. The judge asked, "how long have you been married?"

"About twenty years," replied Mulla.

"You mean you have been married for twenty years and you don't even know your wife's name?"

"Well you see your honor," explained Nasrudin, "we never paid much attention to each other."

KEY

This story is an unfortunate (but often times true) representation of how much people can take each other for granted.

On the other hand, since Nasrudin is in the process of divorcing his wife, maybe his lower self has become such a complete stranger to him, through his self-mortification and spiritual detachment, that it is no longer a real factor in his life.

95

MULLA'S SECRETS

Nasrudin was asked, "Who do you tell your secrets to?"

He replied, "Since people's hearts are not the same as mine, I do not tell my secrets to anyone."

KEY

Since no two hearts are the same, Nasrudin's statement is the best on how to keep a secret. Just don't tell anyone and your secret remains what it is.

(And your central secret is your unique relationship with God, which remains a secret not because it *won't* be told, but because it *can't* be told.)

96

SEVEN-YEAR-OLD VINEGAR

Once, someone asked Nasrudin, "Mulla, I hear that you have some seven-year-old vinegar. Is that true?"

"Yes," replied Mulla.

"Wow! Seven-year-old vinegar is so rare. May I have some?"

"No, I think not," replied Nasrudin. "If I wanted to give my vinegar away, it would not have aged even a month much less seven years."

KEY

There is a difference between being stingy and exercising control over one's desire to spend. If you give things away, they will not last long enough to build up any value. But once something has matured and developed value, it has to be spent responsibly.

And the stronger the vinegar, the less of it is needed to produce the same effect. Keeping one's vinegar to oneself is a little like closing all twenty-eight doors in story number 7. The wise soul is not over-eager to be tasted and found sweet by just anybody who comes along. Sourness can symbolize discretion, and also the power of preservation.

97

THE LOST DONKEY

One day, Mulla lost his donkey. The entire time he looked for the poor beast, he continuously thanked God. Some people came up to him and asked why he was thanking God even though his donkey was gone.

"You see," he replied, "if I had been riding the donkey, I would be lost now and someone else would be looking for me."

KEY

Nasrudin is not the only person who has been guilty of not being able to tell himself from his possessions. Furthermore, there is a great difference between being annihilated in God and simply losing oneself in thoughts, concerns and outer events.

98

THE SIZE OF THE WORLD

A group of people gathered around Mulla Nasrudin and asked him the size of the world. Before Mulla had a chance to answer, a group of people came by carrying a casket toward the graveyard. Nasrudin pointed to the casket and said, "Ask that question of that man. He has seen the entire world and is now leaving."

KEY

Keeping death in mind is one sure way to keep things in perspective. Death also gives a very good scale with which to measure actions and importance.

And this story also has another meaning: The true nature of the world, the 'size' of it, is known only to those who have died to the world. They alone know its secret—a secret that cannot be told in any of the world's languages.

99

HEAVEN AND HELL

Nasrudin was asked, "How long will the human race last?"

"So long as heaven and hell have more room."

KEY

Ask a silly question with no answer, and you deserve whatever answer you get. Heaven and hell will never run out of room; the capacity of the human race—and of any member of it—for good and evil is potentially inexhaustible.

100

A MAN'S WORLD
REMAINS THE SAME

Mulla was asked how old he was. To this he replied that he was forty. Ten years went by and the same question was asked. Again, Mulla replied that he was forty. "How can you be forty?" asked his interrogator. "You said you were forty ten years ago."

"Yes that's's true," replied Nasrudin, "and if you ask me in an-other ten years, I will still be forty. A man does not go back on his words!"

KEY

Misapplication of principle is a common mistake in logic. It also happens regularly in real life situations. Many people confuse stubbornness with consistency, whereas real consistency is to be true to the moment, not to the fixed idea.

Yet there is indeed something in us that does not age, something that was not born and will never die. One of the names for it is the *fitrah*, the human essence.

101

THE USEFULNESS OF THE MOON

Someone asked, "Of the two, which is more useful, the sun or the moon?"

Nasrudin replied, "This question has an obvious answer. The sun comes out during day time when there is no need for its light. But the moon! It comes out and shines when dark has taken over the world. So obviously, the moon is much more beneficial."

KEY

In a way, this story illustrates paying attention to what seems important while missing the reality of the big picture.

In another way, it is simply true. The sun symbolizes God; as it says in the Qur'an, *God is the light of the heavens and the earth.* He gives life to everything, but He cannot be 'used'; He is much too exalted to be employed as a tool in our little works or a strategy in our little schemes. What truly *is* useful is the Revelation by which the light of the divine sun descends into the darkness of our souls, and the spiritual Path by which we ascend and return to the Source of this Revelation.

102

HOT WEATHER

Once, during a gathering, Mulla heard a group of people discussing certain places in the world were it was so hot that the majority of people had to go about naked. Mulla wondered, "How do they differentiate between men and women there?"

KEY

Mulla makes a common mistake of thinking what someone wears (or has, or does for a living) tells you something about the real inner person. And nakedness is also a common symbol for realities that are beyond form entirely. In the Sun of the Unity, all distinctions, all pairs of opposites, are erased.

103

YOUTH

One day, Mulla wanted to mount a horse but was too weak to pull himself up. He said, "Oh youth that has escaped through my fingers." He then looked around and noticed that no one was around. "Between us," he said to himself, "I was not much of anything when I was young."

KEY

One of the advantages of getting old is that you can start blaming your age for things you never had a scapegoat for in the past. Of course, the amount of self-deception involved is open to question.

Another meaning is that, in essence, someone only becomes what he or she already is.

104

KNOWING HOW HE FEELS

Mulla was working on a roof when he fell and was injured. When people came to visit, they asked how he was feeling. He said, "If you really want to know how I feel, you should throw yourself from the roof."

KEY

Some experiences are really not open to communication. This holds for the mystical and the practical.

105

TYING THE HORSE'S REIN

One day, Mulla was sitting outside enjoying some *halwa* when a rider came by. Out of courtesy, and not really expecting him to stop, Mulla asked the rider to join him. Surprisingly, the rider stopped, dismounted and asked Mulla where he could tie his horse's reins. Realizing he would have to share his *halwa*, Mulla replied, "Tie them to my tongue."

KEY

Few things will get you in as much trouble as making an offer you don't expect to be accepted. Before offering, make sure you have thought out what will happen if the offer *is* accepted—especially when you are offering your allegiance to a spiritual Guide. God willing, he will silence you.

GLOSSARY

Akrama: An early disciple of Muhammad who transmitted his teachings to the next generation.

al-Ghazzali: One of the greatest thinkers and philosophers of Islam, and among its foremost theologians. He died in 1111. He lived in the same era as Omar Khayyam.

Attar: Known in the West as the author of *Mantiq at-Tayr* (The Conference of the Birds). He lived in the 12th century.

Baqa': The attainment of divine characteristics and being sustained by God; the stage after *fana'*.

Baraka: Grace, divine favor; also refers to the inner divine gift that leads human beings to the highest levels of enlightenment.

Darvish: Literally, an impoverished person; today it refers to a seeker who has been initiated into a Sufi order.

Dhikr: See *Zekr*.

Fana': The annihilation of human characteristics in God.

Ghaflah: Forgetfulness or negligence, esp. in a spiritual sense.

Hadith: Literally *news*. It generally refers to Prophet Muhammad's teachings. The 'Traditions' of the Prophet Muhammad consist of extra-Qur'anic accounts of his words and deeds, collected and recorded by his followers.

Hal: Literally, the present moment. To Sufis, *hal* refers to the impression of the Divine that enters the heart. It also denotes an ecstatic state.

Halwa: Sweets

Haqiqat: Truth; the destination of someone who follows the spiritual path.

Heraclitus: An ancient Greek philosopher. He saw the world as consisting of basic substances (air, water, earth and fire). His metaphor for the world was that of the river, suggesting that nothing ever really stays the same.

Ibn al-'Arabi: Great Sufi master, born in Andalusia (Muslim Spain), who spent his last years in Damascus. He is sometimes called the Shaykh al-Akbar, 'the greatest master'. And he was perhaps the deepest and most prolific Sufi *writer* of all time. He lived in the 12th and 13th centuries.

I take refuge in God: This phrase is often recited by Muslims when they face evil.

Ibn Abbas: An early disciple of Prophet Muhammad who transmitted his teachings to the next generation.

Islam: A religion based on monotheism, which is considered to be a continuation of Divine teachings that were bestowed upon Moses and Jesus. Its prophet is Muhammad.

Ka'ba: A black cubical building in Mecca symbolizing for Muslims the house of God. It is the goal of a Muslim's pilgrimage, and the direction toward which Muslims turn when praying.

Lower Self: *Nafs* or the ego; the part of the psyche that identifies with the self. The Sufis generally identify four types of *nafs* on the spiritual journey to God: the commanding *nafs* (the passions), the blaming *nafs* (the troubled conscience), the knowing *nafs*, and the *nafs* at rest.

Maqam: Literally means station. It is generally meant as a spiritual station.

Minaret: Tall cylindrical structure. Usually a call to prayer is given from this building.

Muezzin: A person who calls the faithful to prayer.

Mulla: A learned man. Often, it refers to a member of clergy.

Namaz: Muslim prayer [the Persian name; in Arabic, *salat*].

Nafs: see *Lower Self*.

Omar Khayyam: An outstanding mathematician and astronomer, best known in the West for his *Rubaiyat*. He lived in the 11th century.

Rabi'a: A mystic who was born a short time after the death of Muhammad. She lived in the area now called Iraq. She is a major spiritual influence and one of the central figures of the Sufi spiritual tradition.

Ramadan: The month when Muslims fast from dawn to dusk. It is considered to be a holy month when Qur'an was revealed to Prophet Muhammad.

Rumi: Sufi master and the author of *Mathnawi*. He lived in the 13th century.

Shams Tabrizi: Rumi's teacher and mentor.

Sufi: Darvish; one who is initiated into a Sufi order; a seeker who by means of love and devotion moves toward God.

Sufi master: One who guides the aspirants on the Sufi path.

Sufism: A spiritual way of reaching God through the gateway of the heart by means of love; in an outer sense, the practice of the 'organized mystics' of Islam.

Zekr (Dhikr): Remembrance; a practice whereby a Sufi initiate remembers or chants one or many names of God, as directed by the master.

Printed in the United States
130662LV00002B/32/A

9 781597 310703